LIVE LARGE

BE DIFFERENT

SHINE BRIGHT

12 CONTAGIOUS QUALITIES
FOR HEALTHY RELATIONSHIPS

DOUG FIELDS & JOSHUA GRIFFIN

Live Large. Be Different. Shine Bright.
12 Contagious Qualities for Healthy Relationships

Copyright © 2010 Doug Fields

group.com
simplyyouthministry.com

Credits
Authors: Doug Fields and Joshua Griffin
Executive Developer: Nadim Najm
Chief Creative Officer: Joani Schultz
Copy Editor: Rob Cunningham
Cover Art and Production: Veronica Lucas
Production Manager: DeAnne Lear

Unless otherwise indicated, all Scripture quotations are taken from the LIVE Holy Bible, New Living Translation, copyright © 1996, 2004, 2007. Used by permission of Tyndale House Publishers, Inc., Carol Stream, Illinois 60188. All rights reserved.

ISBN 978-0-7644-6319-8

10 9 8 7   18 17 16 15

Printed in the United States of America.

DEDICATION

To the teenagers at Saddleback Church:
Thank you for living large, being different and shining bright
in our community. It is an honor to teach you and watch
you change the world.

To our current and former teenagers—Torie, Cody and Cassie:
You are loved immeasurably and it's exciting to watch you grow
into caring adults.

To our future teenagers—Christian, Austin, Alexis and Jadin:
May you walk with Jesus every day as you grow into the person
God created you to be.

table of contents

INTRODUCTION

INTRODUCTION
by Doug and Josh

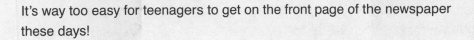

It's way too easy for teenagers to get on the front page of the newspaper these days!

You may be thinking, "What's a newspaper?" Funny. But we old guys still read them, and we've noticed it doesn't take much for a teenager to get noticed. Why is that? Well, we believe it's because adults set the expectation bar so low! If you round up shoes for homeless people or collect a few cans of food for the local shelter or perform some other good deed, you'll make the newspaper.

Those actions are all good and noble! If you're doing good things, by all means, continue. But it's kind of sad that our culture expects so little of teenagers. Honestly, we think teenagers ought to be insulted by low expectations placed on them.

We believe it's time you rise up and do things no one expects. To seize today's opportunities and change the future by the way you live. We want to challenge you to live large, be different, and shine bright. That's what Jesus taught in the Sermon on the Mount, and he wasn't just speaking to adults—his message matters to all of his followers, no matter how young or old.

This book tackles 12 character qualities that will help you live large, be different, and shine bright. Obviously, we could have written a whole lot more, but we wanted to focus on some of the traits that are rarely taught at church. We hope your church is different, but in many churches, people assume that you'll automatically adopt these qualities as soon as you begin following Jesus. Unfortunately, it doesn't happen automatically—developing important character qualities requires time, thought, focus, and intention. Our prayer is that what you read will cause you to think about how you might live large, shine bright, and be different.

We wrote this book as two friends who love Jesus, hang out with teenagers, and dream about what would happen if teenagers were more intentional about their spiritual and personal growth. We had a lot of fun writing this. And about halfway through the book, we realized that it was getting obnoxious when we tried to explain whose illustration was whose. Then we thought, "Who cares?" So instead of writing "I (Josh) ate four burgers" and "I (Doug) drove a car into a wall," we ditched using our names and assumed you wouldn't care. (When we felt like it was important to add our name, we did.)

Our prayer is that the qualities discussed in this book will help you become someone who reflects more of what Jesus spoke about when he said, *"You are the light of the world—like a city on a hilltop that cannot be hidden. No one lights a lamp and then puts it under a basket! Instead, a lamp is placed on a stand, where it gives light to everyone in the house. In the same way, let your good deeds shine out for all to see, so that everyone will praise your heavenly Father" (Matthew 5:14-16 NLT).*

As followers of Jesus we are called to be the light of the world. What a challenge! And what an opportunity! We beg you to live a life that shines bright—and in doing so, you will be different and will live larger than those who don't. Notice why Jesus wants you to be the light—not to live large for your own glory or recognition, but so that others will praise your heavenly Father. That's the goal!

We believe in you!

Doug Fields & Josh Griffin

> In a world of half-truths and outright lies, Jesus calls us to a life of truth. Will you take on the challenge? You *can* handle the truth.

1 INTEGRITY
The Pursuit of Truth

One of my life goals is to be a man of integrity. I want to be someone who is different and lives large. I'm guessing you do too—which is great!

Just so we're on the same page here (and since you're reading this book, I hope we are), the definition I'm using for the word "integrity" is the one synonymous with honesty, trustworthiness, and faithfulness. I'm sure you'd agree that someone who possesses these character qualities is worthy of admiration, especially in an age of declining morals and standards. A person with integrity shines bright in the midst of darkness.

You may also agree that the specific quality of integrity that seems most difficult to maintain is honesty.

We are faced with multiple decisions each day—both large and small—that require us to choose between doing right and wrong, telling the truth or lying, or deciding whether or not to keep a secret. Here's a personal example.

Not too long ago, in the space of just a few hours, I was faced with three decisions that forced me to draw upon my rising reserves of integrity. Early one morning an organization called to inform me they were going to send a check for $1,485, since I had sent them a check for $1,500 instead of $15. A quick glance at my personal records proved they had simply put the decimal point in the wrong place and posted the wrong amount—to my advantage.

To be honest (which is important for a chapter on integrity, right?) I did think about how nice it would be to have the extra cash in my pocket. After all, they made the mistake, not me. I even visualized the laptop computer I had been lusting over for months, the one way out of my price range. How nice it would be to write my books on that! They would probably sell much better, and then more people would learn about Jesus. Hey! Maybe I could view that free money as a "gift" from the Lord! (OK, maybe not! Those thoughts definitely lacked integrity.)

A few hours later, I discovered that my car had been broken into, and that my stereo had been stolen. When I called my insurance agent I was told that all they needed from me was a list of what had been stolen, and they would reimburse me. I wondered, "Just think how easy it would be to say that there were all kinds of things in the car that actually weren't there and add a couple hundred dollars to the price of the stereo. They would never know…right? As a matter of fact, how would they know whether or not I stored my golf clubs in my trunk, or if I even played golf?" I tried to justify my thoughts by saying that I had been ripped off, so why not rip off someone else? "Insurance is so expensive," I reasoned, "so why not get something for all of the money I had been paying every month?" It would have been easy to do, but it would have lacked integrity.

That same evening my wife and I went to the theater to see an early movie. After it ended, we bumped into some friends in the lobby who invited us to join them for the film they were about to see. Of course, since we didn't pay for the second movie, it could have been viewed as stealing if we did walk in. But since we were already in the theater lobby where no one was taking tickets, it would have been very easy to do.

Decisions. Decisions. Decisions. Those were just three of my examples. Now take a minute to think of all of the daily (and hourly!) decisions you face that require you to determine if you'll be honest or not. It isn't always easy to make the right choices, is it? I know it isn't easy for me! For example, I completely blew it on one of the three decisions I just wrote about. Of course, I felt lousy afterward (especially because I knew beforehand that what I was going to do was wrong) and the guilt I experienced wasn't worth it! Besides, the second movie wasn't even close to being as good as the one I paid for.

But the truth is, even though it can be challenging at times to make the right decisions, those of us who choose to follow Jesus need to pursue his example as well.

JESUS SPEAKS OUT ON INTEGRITY

Jesus was clear and concise when he spoke of integrity in Matthew 5:37 (NIV): "Simply let your 'Yes' be 'Yes,' and your 'No,' 'No.'" In other words, speak the truth. In doing so, others will learn to trust and believe you.

One day after reading Jesus' words (let your "yes" be "yes" and your "no" be "no"), I decided to count how many times I didn't speak the *absolute* truth. I was amazed—and more than a little embarrassed—at the results. Of course, none of the things I said were meant to be harmful displays of dishonesty. In fact, most were quite the opposite.

For example, I would see one of my friends at school and say, "Hey is that a new shirt? It looks great!" Yet in the back of my mind I would be thinking, "Dude, put that blouse back in your mom's closet!" Or I would say, "I'm so grateful for the invitation to your party, it sounds like a lot of fun, but my grandparents are flying in from Colorado" even though I really did not want to go to the party. I was continually catching myself trying to find ways around the absolute truth. This has been a struggle of mine for a long time, and it may have been for you as well.

When I struggle with something, I'll eventually try to figure something specific to help me in my struggle. For example, when I told my wife about my truth-telling experiment, we came up with the idea of an integrity beeper that would help us hold each other accountable in our pursuit of being absolute truth-tellers and people of integrity. Fortunately, there were no wires or electricity involved. It was simple: Every time either one of us would say or do something that was not completely honest, the other person would make a "beep" sound to remind us that we had fallen short. For example, I might have said, "Jake, thanks for dropping over; it was great timing" and my wife would "beep" because she knew Jake had come by at a time when I really needed to get something done. We have a lot of fun with this system and although we treat it like a little game, it's a helpful reminder of how easy it is to stray from the truth (Although, for some reason, my wife tends to beep more than I do. Hmm.)

We wanted to begin the book with this specific chapter because we hang out with a lot of teenagers who struggle with integrity issues and yet they want to live large, be different, and shine bright. But you don't do any of those if you're known as a person who lacks integrity.

Let's first take a look at what can result when we lack integrity, and then focus on some realistic actions to take to aid us in becoming the honest men and women that Jesus intends for us to be as we follow him.

"But those who do what is right come to the light so others can see that they are doing what God wants" (John 3:21 NLT).

RESULTS OF LACKING INTEGRITY

Lies Create Guilt

For the vast majority of us, dishonest behavior brings feelings of guilt. Guilt is a powerful feeling that invades our minds and often causes us to feel as if we are worthless. Guilt is like a tiny Ultimate Fighter living inside of us. Every time we are dishonest, he beats us up, causing great pain and tension. Although medical and psychological experts don't always agree on why we experience guilt, the cold, hard fact is that we do, and it can be an emotional, spiritual, and physical drain on those who are trying to follow Jesus.

Lies Lead to More Lies... Hope You Have a Good Memory

There's an old saying that goes something like this: "If you always tell the truth, you never have to remember what you said." When I was in high school I knew of a guy who actually kept a small notebook with him at all times to record his "stories," simply so he could remember to whom he had told what lies. Crazy, right? I think he may have gone on to write for the National Enquirer. Unfortunately, his system didn't work, and he jeopardized his relationships when his friends found out that they had been lied to for a long time. Even with all the latest technology and recording devices, it would be an incredible chore to store and file all your lies just so you would not get caught up in them. It just wouldn't be worth it!

I learned very early that lies have a way of catching up with us. I once told my parents that I was going to spend the night at Bob King's house, and (you guessed it) Bob told his parents that he was going to spend the night at mine. We then took two small lounge chairs and jumped the fence of a nearby drive-in movie, where we were going to spend most of our evening. (Ever heard of a drive-in theater? If not, Google it. They were fun—but apparently not profitable.) Before the first movie was over we bumped into Bob's older brother and quickly made up the story that we were there with my parents. After the movie, we went to sleep in our new fort near the riverbed so we could get up early in the morning for the best fishing (I know, very Mark Twain-ish).

When we returned to our homes later the next day, our parents acted as if nothing was out of the ordinary. We each told another little lie about the great time we had at the other friend's home, and they let us dig ourselves deeper and deeper into the black hole we'd created the night before. Little did we know that the night before, Bob's older brother called to ask my older sister a question, and you can guess how things progressed from that point! We had told so many different lies that Bob and I could not even remember the real story. I would have rather been anywhere in the world instead of standing (squirming, really) where I was, trying to talk my way out of that mess. Dishonesty has a way of getting us in trouble no matter how smart we think we are.

The wicked are trapped by their own words, but the godly escape such trouble (Proverbs 12:13 NLT).

We Begin to Believe Lies

I've done my share of counseling other people through the years as a pastor, and I have found that people who have trouble telling the truth actually begin to believe their own lies. Even if you confront them with all kinds of evidence, they look at you as if you were the liar.

People who continually lie create masks that keep others from knowing the truth, but the masks also keep them from becoming the people God created them to be. They may think a mask provides protection, but it's actually a trap. People become comfortable telling lies—but then they can't escape the trouble those lies bring. In the end, they compound the problem with more lies to keep the truth from being known.

People who lie compulsively and who no longer know whether or not they are telling the truth are often called pathological liars; they have an emotional problem. Do you know someone like this? Could you possibly be this someone? Would you tell me the truth if I asked you in person?

Followers of Jesus are not immune to lying. But a Christian on a journey toward spiritual maturity, should strive to make integrity a quality of his or her life. As this becomes one of your goals in your desire to live large, be different, and shine bright, don't be surprised at other Christians who struggle with lying. They are human, just like you, and conquering lying can be a process.

> ***Don't lie to each other, for you have stripped off your old sinful nature and all its wicked deeds. Put on your new nature, and be renewed as you learn to know your Creator and become like him (Colossians 3:9-10 NLT).***

Lying Affects Others

When we tell lies, we are often doing so to look good or to avoid some type of pain or trouble. We rarely think of the consequences that others experience when they somehow become entwined in our lies. Friends may wind up lying to help protect our original lie just because they cherish our friendship. I would even say that many of us might expect a true friend to lie for us. I once heard a story of a young boy who was told by his mother that when the phone rang, to answer it and tell whoever it was that she was in the bathtub. So the little boy dutifully answered the phone and not wanting to lie said, "We don't have a bathtub, but that's where Mom is."

Another way we can affect others with our speech is by carelessly talking about them. This is gossip, and the negative effect that it can have on another person's life is unbelievable! I have seen relationships broken and people emotionally devastated simply because someone decided to talk about another person behind their back. This is a very harmful and destructive action.

> ***Telling lies about others is as harmful as hitting them with an ax, wounding them with a sword, or shooting them with a sharp arrow (Proverbs 25:18 NLT).***

Most of us like to be "people in the know" or "in the loop" who are up on the latest information about other people. Because of that, one of your friends may hear something about someone and relay that information to you. And that information will most likely cause you to judge the person who was the subject of the gossip. You move into judging because you think what you heard is truth. But gossip is like judging the beauty of a 500-piece puzzle by looking at only five pieces of it. Put simply, your desire to be "in the know" shouldn't be used as an excuse to engage in gossip. If you're not part of the problem or part of the solution, it's gossip.

STEPS LEADING TO INTEGRITY

Even if we are fully aware of the pitfalls of lying and gossip, it remains difficult to maintain our integrity. It becomes increasingly hard to be honest when we feel that the truth will make us look bad, or when the lie is so small that we believe we will never get caught, or even when we think that there is no way we will get by without being dishonest.

I believe with all my heart that there is a road to recovery if you share in this common struggle. Here are four ideas to help you focus on being a person of integrity.

Admit Your Problem

One of the first steps to overcoming a lack of integrity is to admit to yourself that you have a problem; you are no better than other people who struggle with this common issue. I have counseled many teenagers who are unwilling to admit that they may have a problem. Many feel that by confessing they are "lowering" themselves, and that they are going to look bad. My opinion is that this mentality (not wanting to look bad) is the primary reason for the problem in the first place.

It takes a strong person to be able to admit a failing! Several years ago, Lyndsey, a girl in my youth group, had a secret struggle with drinking and drugs. She would come home at least three times a week either drunk or stoned but was still unable to admit she had a problem.

One night at 3:30 a.m. Lyndsey called me from a party and asked me if I could come pick her up. When I arrived at the house, I found her passed out on the bathroom floor lying in her own vomit. The next morning she told me she was finally ready to admit her problem and wanted help. Lyndsey checked herself into a drug rehabilitation hospital to recover from the sickness that had begun to dominate her life. Today, her one and only life has been changed forever because she was strong enough to admit she had a problem.

Can you be as willing as Lyndsey to admit that you have a problem? What if that problem is in the area of honesty or integrity? Are you willing to admit you may have a problem?

Ask Someone to Hold You Accountable

If you have a problem with honesty, you need to honestly admit it to yourself, but to really get healthy you should consider sharing your struggle with a friend. That friend can become a key factor in helping you pursue integrity. I know this is scary and I know firsthand how difficult this is to do!

Who is someone who knows you best and spends the most time with you? Ask him or her to help you adopt a version of the integrity beeper system I described earlier in the chapter. It is really a helpful reminder! (In Chapter 6 on Transparency we discuss how it is essential to have a friend with whom you can share anything, even your faults and struggles.)

Ask God for Truth

God is the source of truth. If we want truth to illuminate our lives, we need to go to God through Jesus, and he promises us we will find it. Jesus said, *"I am the way and the truth and the life. No one comes to the Father except through me" (John 14:6 NIV)*. Ask God to be a vital part in the process of pursuing integrity. Pray constantly and know that God not only hears your prayers, but he also wants you to grow into maturity as a follower of Jesus. Jesus said, *"I came to bring truth to the world. All who love the truth are my followers" (John 18:37 TLB).*

Remember You Are in a Process

Throughout this book, we will constantly remind you that this life of following Jesus is a process. You will not wake up tomorrow without faults. Even if you read this entire book, you'll still be in the process of becoming more like Jesus. You're not going to be just like Jesus (sinless) as long as you're alive on this planet, but don't be discouraged. Becoming a person of integrity will reveal both victories and failures; this is a natural part of inner character change!

Much of my life as a follower of Jesus can be summed up with this phrase: *Three Steps Forward, Two Steps Back.* That's my life in a nutshell. I'm guessing you can relate. You start strong in your desire to be like Jesus and you move three steps forward, but then you mess up (and lack the truth) and move two steps back. The good news about growing as a follower of Jesus is that you'll slowly gain one step in the process. And each one of those is one step closer to maturity in Christ.

Keep stepping toward integrity!

LIVING LARGE TODAY

Use these questions for a time of reflection, as you write in your personal journal, or when you get together with your small group.

1. You find an envelope with $500 cash inside it while shopping at the mall. What do you do?

2. Think of a time recently when your integrity was tested. Did you win or lose that test?

3. Rate yourself on an integrity scale of 1 to 10 (1 being the lowest, 10 being the highest). What steps might you take to increase that number?

4. Who in your life is currently holding you accountable to become a person of integrity? If there is no one, consider writing down a name and asking that person to play a vital role in your life. If you do have someone like that, take a minute to call or text him/her a "thank you" for their help in your life.

> There are positive people and energy drainers—who are you going to become? No matter what you face, a positive, optimistic attitude will make you more attractive and someone others will want to be around.

2 ENTHUSIASM
The Contagiousness of Happiness

I love being around enthusiastic people—it's fun! They have such a positive outlook on life, and they make me want to be enthusiastic too.

I spend a lot of time in front of crowds, congregations, and audiences, so I have ample opportunity to study the faces of people. Sure, I see smiles and hear laughter, but I also frequently see people who appear to be depressed, lonely, or simply hiding behind a mask. Sadly, it's a rare moment when I come across someone who truly bubbles with a genuine, enthusiastic attitude. When you encounter enthusiastic people, they simply stand out in the crowd (different than people who are obnoxious or wild) because, no matter the situation, they radiate their own private ray of sunshine.

Imagine for a second what it would be like if we had to wear digital signs around our necks that flashed a description of our moods to the people around us. The enthusiastic person would have a sign that flashed: "I love life," "It's great to be alive!" or "YES!" These messages are attractive! Yet the reverse is also true! There are some teenagers in my youth group whose signs would read: "I guess it's just another day," "I'm bored," "I don't care," or simply, "ZZZZZZ." These teenagers are difficult to be around.

What would your sign say?

Regardless of how you might rate yourself on an enthusiasm scale, there is always opportunity to grow. In this chapter we will look at how enthusiasm can help you live large, shine bright, and be different—and, what you can do to become a more enthusiastic person.

WHAT ENTHUSIASM CAN DO FOR YOU

Enthusiasm is Contagious
It's really simple: When you're around enthusiastic people, you tend to become enthusiastic.

When I was in college, I took a class called "Recreation and Camping." I registered for this class for two simple reasons: 1) it sounded easy, and 2) even though it met at the dreadful hour of 8:00 a.m., odds were I could probably sleep in often and not miss out on much material.

I went the first day of class to pick up the course outline and see if my suspicions were correct. As I sat in the cold, damp room with 15 other yawning students, I tried to figure out what the professor would be like since no one knew him.

Suddenly, this bigger-than-life man galloped in (yes…galloped) with a smile larger than all the outdoors and made a beeline straight for my desk. I'll never forget it. I thought for a moment, "He's figured out my slothful intentions for this class, and I am so busted." But instead, he extended his huge right hand out to me and said, "Good morning! My name is Wayne Tesch. My friends call me Wayne!"

"Hi, I'm Doug Fields," I said, sitting up a little straighter in my seat.

"Doug, I'm THRILLED you are in this class!"

Wayne then went to each of the other students and repeated that same greeting. This man lived large!

You should have seen how the energy of that classroom changed! His enthusiasm was contagious…even at 8 a.m.! Sixteen pairs of eyes (sorry, I don't remember how many students wore glasses) were glued to him for the remainder of the hour. If there had been a digital sign around his neck, his enthusiasm would have overloaded the circuits with the message of "I'm worth following! My ideas are good! You are valuable to me! Let's celebrate life together!"

I never missed one of his classes. In fact, as the semester went on, I invited several of my friends to come with me (and believe me, they were as fond of 8 a.m. classes as I originally was), just so they could experience the power and joy of his amazing attitude. I told them, "You have got to see this guy teach. He makes school and learning fun. It is unbelievable!"

Wayne Tesch's enthusiasm impacted my life and the lives of many students in that class. I learned the contagious nature of enthusiasm from a man I intended to sleep through!

Enthusiasm Helps Us Reach Goals

My youth pastor taught me this phrase when I was a teenager: "He who aims at nothing gets there every time." I believe this is not only true, but is a helpful motivator behind goal setting. If you are a goal setter (and, if not, I would encourage you to become one) then you are always trying to figure out the best steps to reaching your goals.

Enthusiasm might be one of the first steps you take to achieve a goal. If you are excited about reaching a realistic goal, then there is little that can stop you. Enthusiasm is a powerful motivator. In fact, I would revise my youth pastor's quote slightly to make it a little more positive and just as accurate by saying, "He who aims with enthusiasm gets there every time."

Financier Charles M. Schwab once said, "A man can succeed at almost anything for which he has unlimited enthusiasm."

Enthusiasm Attracts People

This sure has been true in my life! As I mentioned earlier, I am attracted to those who possess enthusiasm. Think about who you would really choose to be around if you could—really think about it. What is it you like about them? I may be wrong, but most likely they are positive people who are enthusiastic about life. Negative people are draining and are typically no fun to be around, while enthusiasm seems to have magnetic capabilities that quickly attract others.

When my friend Donna began dating David (now her husband) we got together for lunch to talk about her new and exciting relationship. It was easy to be sincerely excited for Donna and the new things that were happening in her life because she was so enthusiastic about David. Her enthusiasm was attractive and contagious, and I found myself being excited to know more about her relationship.

As we were walking to our car after lunch, she told me how very thankful she was that I was so excited and interested in her life. It was so easy to be excited because I just fed off of her enthusiasm. That lunch conversation was a positive boost in our friendship because ever since, she has trusted me with all her new and exciting adventures. My enthusiasm for her situation deepened what was already a good friendship.

Take a second and think about this—do people walk away from time with you refreshed and excited, or drained and exhausted?

Enthusiasm Sells

The best salespeople in the world are those who not only believe in their product, but are enthusiastic about its potential impact for the consumer. Would you buy something from someone who said, "You probably wouldn't want to buy this—would you?" No way! We tend to buy from confident and enthusiastic people. Even infomercials understand this principle very well. I should know—I've bought six ShamWows, a bottle of miracle car polish, and a Magic Bullet blender all because the salespeople were so enthusiastic. They drew me in!

When I was a kid playing baseball in Little League, I had to sell 50 overpriced, high-calorie candy bars in order to earn a uniform. My plan was simple: All I had to do was go to 25 houses and sell two bars per house. That uniform would be mine in no time!

Unfortunately, what I <u>didn't</u> include in my brilliant plan was an enthusiastic sales pitch. Needless to say, I learned a hard lesson that day. After 25 houses, I had sold only one bar (to my best friend's mom, who later told me that she gave the candy bar to the dog). I stumbled home crying, planning to quit Little League because without a uniform, I would have to play in my Superman underwear.

After my parents picked me up off the floor, they asked me to tell them my sales pitch. Surprised, I told them I just went up to the door, grunted a little bit, held the candy bar out, and raised my eyebrows as if to say, "You wouldn't want these candy bars would you?"

After witnessing my pathetic plea, my parents sprung into action, infusing the sales' pitch with the ability of a presidential speech writer. My dad taped my practice speech so I could watch it back and coached me on smiles and enthusiastic voice inflections and gestures. It took a little practice, but I soon became good! Later, my justifiably proud parents stood at the front door as I raced down the street to attack (I mean, serve) the neighborhood once again. Nineteen houses later (which may still be a Little League candy bar-selling record) I raced home empty-handed (which is a good thing when you're selling stuff). Even better, my pockets were bulging with uniform money. I learned a lesson about the power of enthusiasm.

Enthusiasm helps to sell not only products but also yourself. Enthusiasm helps when interviewing for a job, making first impressions, and communicating a message to another person.

Enthusiasm Can Change Your Life

I've already listed some specific life-changing features of enthusiasm, so let's do a quick review. Enthusiasm can improve your attitude, build confidence, relieve fears, help you with a job or school work, make you a better athlete, help you appreciate life, bring you closer to God, and much, much more. As a matter of fact, I'd like to hear someone try to make an argument against being enthusiastic.

If I have helped you see some of the positive changes enthusiasm can bring about for you, then read on to see how you might become a more enthusiastic person. If you still aren't sold on enthusiasm, you may need to start this chapter over again.

BECOMING MORE ENTHUSIASTIC

Start and End Each Day with an Enthusiastic Attitude

If we could tattoo these words of the psalmist on our hearts, two things would happen. First, it would hurt like crazy. But second, we would surely become more enthusiastic people. Here's a simple exercise that can bookend each of your days with enthusiasm.

> *This is the day the Lord has made; let us rejoice and be glad in it (Psalm 118:24 NLT).*

Each morning when you wake up, repeat this verse in anticipation of a great day. Then, before you go to bed, thank God for the day you were given, and pray that you might wake the next day with an enthusiasm about life and an excitement for the God who created it.

Think Enthusiastically

Your mind is an incredible gift from God. It holds the potential to help you to be the person he intended you to be. After you pray for your day, imagine yourself having a positive attitude as you picture all the people you may see, the conversations you will have, and the places you will go—in short, everything God has planned for your day. You will find that you will be drawn to the results you've pictured in your mind. This is one of my favorite mental exercises, and I do it all the time.

God gave us minds, so let's use them to help us be more enthusiastic people.

Do Not Overload Your Life

I am writing out of weakness rather than strength in this area. I know firsthand that it is difficult to be enthusiastic when you are tired. The longer I'm around teenagers, the more I notice them being tired. Teenagers are busy, and busy people get tired. We recently surveyed our teenagers asking for topics that they were most interested in, and the number one response was "stress."

For example, there's a girl in my youth group who is on the swim team and drill team, takes dance lessons, is involved in school government, teaches Sunday School, has a part-time job, and is part of our high school leadership on top of her normal school class load. One day, her parents came to me wondering why she is so lethargic in relationships and around the house. I had to open their eyes to the fact that their daughter is burning herself out and has no time to be enthusiastic about anything. Do you know anyone like her?

For enthusiasm to become a vital part of your everyday life, you may need to prioritize your activities so that you leave some untapped energy for the things that are most important to you.

Realize Enthusiasm Comes When You Are Connected to God

The word "enthusiasm" comes from the Greek words *en theos*, which actually means "in God." I believe that God is the source of energy, vitality, and power for those who have come into a relationship with him through his Son Jesus Christ. We read in Scripture: *God created everything through him, and nothing was created except through him (John 1:3 NLT)*, and *"For in him (God) we live and move and have our being" (Acts 17:28a NIV)*.

Commit a New Image of What/Who You Want to Be to God

Through prayer, tell God that you dearly desire to be a more enthusiastic person. Since enthusiasm is found "in God," keep plugging your life into the Creator of life, continually asking him to mold you into the enthusiastic person you want to become. *Delight yourself in the Lord, and he will give you the desires of your heart (Psalm 37:4 NIV).* With God being the ultimate source of enthusiasm, there is no better way to seek enthusiasm than through him.

There is a special contagious nature with enthusiasm. It has the power to change your life and the lives of the people around you. Be challenged to work through these steps toward enthusiasm so you can also possess this unique quality.

LIVING LARGE TODAY

Use these questions for a time of reflection, as you write in your personal journal, or when you get together with your small group.

1. Think about a few of your friends: Are they positive or negative people? Why are you attracted to them?

2. Can you think of a recent situation in your life when enthusiasm would have changed the outcome?

3. From what you learned in this chapter, how might you start and end your day with God? How do you think these exercises might change things?

4. Is your schedule too busy? Is it robbing you of joy? What might you cut from your schedule? What's keeping you from doing it?

Conflict is a difficult but necessary part of life. Learning how to handle it now will allow you to live at peace with everyone and be different in all your relationships. Learn how to argue in a way that is right and honoring.

3 MANAGING CONFLICT
The Tough Road to Better Relationships

My friend has a favorite saying that is both accurate and brutal: "Life is tough, and then you die." Some could argue this, but for many people life seems to go from tension, to conflict, to trauma, with an occasional detour into intense agony. You may escape some harsh pain, but everyone can expect some conflict and tension in every close, long-term relationship. Your degree of tension may vary with the circumstances, but the tension is still tension and it's never fun.

Most of us experience relational conflict and suffer because we don't fully take the time to deal with tension when it first arises. Tension can grow like mold on stale bread (remember that experiment in school, right?) until it just consumes us. When that happens, we can overreact or make irrational decisions or statements that we often regret.

However, many of us would rather eat raw liver or get our teeth drilled by an unlicensed plumber than deal with the source of our tension. Instead, we keep everything inside and don't let anyone know how we feel. Unfortunately, neither exploding at others nor simmering inside is an effective way to manage tension and conflict. These methods won't produce any positive results for our relationships. In fact, they actually bring more tension.

This chapter is a little different from the others: It's interesting! (Just kidding—seeing if you're still paying attention or if you've drifted off thinking about a tension that you're currently experiencing.) But seriously, we will first take a look at some examples of conflict in the Bible and then work through a "conflict cycle" to better understand conflict and how we might deal with it. Even though dealing with conflict can be difficult, how we choose to handle it can show the people around us just how "different" our life is.

BIBLICAL CONFLICT

Unresolved Conflicts

Life typically works best when conflicts are resolved as soon as possible. When we don't take the time to resolve them, we can set the stage for very painful experiences, and the pain is usually ours. When we choose not to deal with the source of disagreements, we can carry around feelings that gnaw at us. And here's a funny thing: the people with whom we have conflicts often know nothing about the weight we are carrying. We feel conflict and they walk around not feeling our pain.

When I was a freshman in high school, one of my friends made up a nickname for me that wasn't very flattering. No, I'm not telling you what it was. It seems silly, but it really made me mad when he used this name for me (still not telling). Of course, since my other friends laughed when he said it, I pretended that it was funny too. But as the name-calling continued (stop asking me), I found myself staying away from this guy, not because he was a jerk, but because I simply had a hard time confronting him with my true and hurt feelings.

At a church retreat during our senior year, I finally told him that it really bothered me when he called me this name. His response was, "You should have told me. I would have stopped." I learned a BIG lesson that day. For almost four years I kept a potential friendship from developing because I was afraid to share my feelings. I experienced four years of internal pain and he didn't feel anything.

Conflict may arise for any number of reasons: jealousy, self-centeredness, possessiveness, personality clashes, and even simple misunderstandings. Unresolved conflict often affects us emotionally and spiritually. But no matter what causes the conflict, it needs to be dealt with in a manner that will save the relationship and enable everyone concerned to continue with the process of life.

No one is free from conflict, not even the great people in the Bible. Conflict started in the beginning of our history (see Genesis 3; 4; 6:13; 11:5-9). There are many conflicts described in the New Testament as well, some involving the Apostle Paul and even our Savior Jesus.

Jesus' Involvement in Conflicts

It may be hard for us to imagine that Jesus (the Prince of Peace) was involved in conflicts, but it is true. In Matthew 21:12-17 we read that Jesus stirred up trouble when he entered the Temple and physically threw out the merchants who were buying and selling items in the courtyard. Another time, he played the peacemaker for a woman who had been caught in adultery (see John 8:3-11). Of course, there were many times when Jesus avoided conflict and went his own way (see Luke 4:28-30).

But the fact remains that Jesus didn't simply avoid conflicts during his time on earth, and yet he continued to have an effective ministry in spite of all the situations surrounding him.

Paul and Barnabas' Conflict

One of the most well known conflicts in the New Testament involved two God-honoring men who couldn't agree on what they should do in their ministry. The conflict was between Paul and Barnabas, and the story is found in Acts 15:36-41.

Paul and Barnabas had already done a lot of ministry together, and they were planning on traveling again to tell others about Jesus when they disagreed on who else should come along on their next journey. Barnabas wanted to bring his cousin John Mark along and Paul didn't. We don't know all the details, but Paul may have been mad at John Mark because he had abandoned them during their previous trip. It seems that Barnabas wanted to give John Mark another chance, and Paul didn't. The Bible says that there was a sharp disagreement between Paul and Barnabas, and they went their separate ways (see v. 39). Paul chose Silas to be his companion, and they traveled extensively establishing and strengthening churches (see v. 41).

It is important to note that although there was a good deal of tension in their disagreement, Paul and Barnabas dealt with it and continued on with what God had planned for them (encouraging and strengthening churches). They provide us a great example for us to pattern our actions after, especially when dealing with our fellow followers of Jesus.

Conflict Cycle

Once you acknowledge that it is natural for conflicts to arise throughout your lifetime, you can focus on finding practical ways to work through them with the least amount of pain and the greatest rewards.

Below is a simple chart of a potential conflict cycle that may help you to see where you are during a given conflict. As you look this over, it can help you reach your ultimate goal. This is just one way to understand conflict better:

Tension
(start here)

Resolution

Asking Questions

Making adjustments

PEACE

Gathering ammunition

Confrontation

Tension

All conflicts begin somewhere. This is where you first experience feelings of tension, for whatever reasons, and feel that there is some type of friction in your relationship. At this point your feelings come into play and you may feel hurt, betrayed, or misunderstood.

Questioning

This is the stage when you begin to ask yourself questions. "Is this tension my fault?" "Do I have the right to feel this way?" "What did I do to deserve this?" Basically you are trying to figure out the reasons you feel the way you do. In an ideal world, this is the best place to attempt to resolve your conflict. Ask the other person the questions you've been asking yourself. It's fine to be naive, but make sure you have an attitude of simply wanting to figure out what is going on and not trying to pick a fight. The Bible says we shouldn't end the day angry, so the best time to talk about a conflict is as soon as you can have a rational conversation.

> *And "don't sin by letting anger control you." Don't let the sun go down while you are still angry (Ephesians 4:26 NLT).*

Gathering Ammunition

By the time you reach this stage, you've probably begun thinking of ways to get even or words that would hurt the other person. Depending on how you choose to manage your conflict, at this point your anger can begin to build up toward a great explosion. Or if you're the type who "stuffs" their feelings, you may begin to store your anger away without dealing with it (like I did in the name-calling story). This is a dangerous stage and should be avoided when possible!

Confrontation

This is vital in your conflict cycle. Confrontation means spending time with the other person or people talking about your conflict, and it doesn't have to be a negative experience. Confrontation doesn't have to be synonymous with "battle." Confrontation can be done in a sensitive manner with both sides getting an opportunity to express and explain their feelings. Of course, anytime too much ammunition has been gathered (Step 3), there is a good chance that a "battle" will break out, and defensiveness and separation will be the result. However, if you approach a confrontation in a loving manner and ask fair and caring questions (Step 2), both of you can agree to change and make adjustments, or (as a last resort) mutually decide to walk away from the relationship (kind of like Paul and Barnabas did). Obviously, a resolution leading toward reconciliation is preferred.

Making Adjustments

If the confrontation went well, adjustments must be made so that the relationship can improve, and both parties need to agree on the changes. Expectations need to be discussed. You may find that it will be more beneficial for both of you to do some of the changing so that you are a team in bringing resolution to the conflict. This step requires maturity and humility.

Resolution

This is when the conflict is finally over and you have mutually decided on the next steps in your relationship. You need to realize that you may still have painful feelings, especially if you were hurt. It's OK to still have these feelings, but it is important to let the other person know that you have forgiven them.

Conflict is painful! Confrontation can be even more so. But confrontation is vital to change, and change (in attitude or action) is critical to the resolution of any conflict.

The simple truth is, if we have a pulse and are still breathing, we are going to experience conflict. It's difficult, but it's an integral part of experiencing and developing relationships with other people. God has made many experiences—the joyful and the painful ones—available to us through our relationships with others. It is all part of his design to make us more like Jesus.

If you are going to live large, be different, and shine bright, you can't avoid conflict. When it arrives (and it will) you've got to be able to face it in a way that leads to peace. Peace is a choice—you can choose resentment or you can choose peace. Be different and choose peace!

LIVING LARGE TODAY

Use these questions for a time of reflection, as you write in your personal journal, or when you get together with your small group.

1. Are you in any relational conflict right now? Where are you in the conflict cyle (p. 34)? What questions are you asking about the conflict?

2. What steps do you need to take to make things right within your relationship?

3. What are your greatest fears about trying to resolve conflict in a God-honoring way?

4. Who is someone you can talk to about your actions within this conflict who can hold you accountable to do the right thing?

You hear it said all the time, "It's all about you! Just remain focused on your needs and your wants and you'll get ahead in life." Wait! Could it be that there is more to life than YOU? Life becomes so much different when giving is part of it.

4 GIVING
The Percentage Game

I was recently at a Christian convention where a professional musician gave a concert to nearly 1,500 people. In the middle of her set, she mentioned that she was giving away free CDs to the first 100 people who visited the company's booth after the concert. Without waiting, a mob of people raced to the lobby. They were more concerned about getting a free CD than they were about being rude to the person giving it away.

Surprised? Not really! Sad? Yes, especially since the rude people were followers of Jesus. What triggered the rudeness? The strong desire to look out for Number One. Can you relate to that?

We live in a self-centered society that is all about "Number One." In short, our culture gives birth to takers instead of givers. The media may talk or write about us as "consumers," but that is simply a more gentle word for "takers." We are encouraged to take whatever we can get our hands on because we are entitled to it.

Even Christians get caught up in this selfish attitude. Yet this attitude is in complete opposition to what Jesus modeled and what he expects. God desires for us to be givers, not takers. He wants us to give 100 percent in some areas of our lives and smaller portions in others. But the important point is that followers of Jesus are called to be givers.

GOD WANTS 100 PERCENT OF. . .

...Your Life, Relationships, and Material Possessions

If we are to follow Jesus, then we need to love him more than we love anything or anyone else (see Luke 14:26). The Apostle Paul tells us that we are to present our bodies as living sacrifices to God (see Romans 12:1). These verses clearly indicate that God wants more than a portion; he wants everything, our entire lives.

In the Old Testament, there is an unusual event where God asked Abraham to sacrificially murder his only son, Isaac, whom he loved very much. While it seems harsh, God was testing Abraham's commitment to him. And when God saw that Abraham was actually going to be faithful and obey the command, God interceded and spared Isaac's life and richly blessed Abraham for his faith and obedience (see Genesis 22).

God wants our faith to be like Abraham's—a faith where God becomes Number One. If other things come before our relationship with God, our faith is out of balance. Perfect balance is when we give 100 percent of our lives to God so that he can use us the way he wants us to be used. God is jealous when it comes to having other things placed before him (see Exodus 20:5). That is why it was so important for Abraham to be tested. God desired to use Abraham and wanted to make sure he would be faithful. Because of Abraham's obedience, God used him to become the pioneer of our faith.

Many Christians claim that God is the most important priority in their lives, and yet when it comes down to it they usually give more time and attention to their material possessions and relationships, than to God. I know people who are more excited about their car or the thought of owning a better car than they are about God. Love for their car has become their "Isaac" (the thing that they love more dearly than anything else).

When I stop to evaluate my own relationship with God, I can see that my "Isaac" is often my commitment to human relationships. I often find myself putting my relationship with family and friends before my relationship with God. According to God's Word and his ways, this is wrong!

Whatever our "Isaac" is, it needs to be sacrificed on the altar of faith in order to prove that God is Number One in our lives. God blessed Abraham when it became clear that his faith and obedience were stronger than his love for his only son Isaac. We need to ask ourselves, "Are my possessions and relationships so important to me that I am willing to miss out on blessings from God?"

God wants us to have the faith and obedience of Abraham. He wants us to give up our Isaacs, those things that we love more dearly than anything else, and make him Number One in our lives. That's what it means to give 100 percent!

While it is important to realize that God wants 100 percent in the areas of faith and obedience, there are other areas where he asks for a smaller percentage. He knows that we are capable of giving 100 percent of our lives, relationships, and material possessions, but in the following two areas God seems to settle for a little less. In no way does this mean that God doesn't feel these areas are important. It just shows that a smaller percentage is sufficient to illustrate our obedience to him.

In a broad sense these two areas are interrelated with our life and material possessions of which we are to give 100 percent to God. But in a more defined sense, these specific acts of giving are demonstrations of our 100 percent faith in God.

GOD WANTS A PERCENTAGE OF. . .

...Your Time

There is a principle in the Old Testament called the Sabbath. (We will look at this in greater depth in the chapter on Reflection.) The Sabbath is simply a special 24-hour period of time set aside for God. The observance of the Sabbath was carried into the New Testament, and today there are still people who faithfully observe it.

Originally, this Sabbath time was given to God in worship and in acknowledgement of his greatness, and we can approach it the same way today. How much time do you give to God? How much personal time? How much time do you volunteer to a ministry? God doesn't ask for 100 percent of our time, but he does ask that we give him a percentage of it.

...Your Money

In the Old Testament, people were required by law to give a portion (tithe) of their money. When all of the requirements were added up, they had to give over 20 percent of their income. In the New Testament we find that we are no longer under the law, but are still expected to give of our finances. Under the new covenant of Jesus we are to give as we prosper.

As we grow closer to Jesus it becomes apparent that Jesus is more interested in our heart than our money. One time Jesus got upset with the Pharisees (a group of religious leaders of his day) who seemed to be more concerned about being legalistic about their giving than they were with showing love for God (see Matthew 23:23). Jesus is always more concerned with heart attitude than dollar amount. Here is a beautiful illustration of this point:

Jesus sat down opposite the place where the offerings were put and watched the crowd putting their money into the temple treasury. Many rich people threw in large amounts. But a poor widow came and put in two very small coins, worth only a fraction of a penny. Calling his disciples to him, Jesus said, "I tell you the truth, this poor widow has put more into the treasury than all the others. They all gave out of their wealth; but she, out of her poverty, put in everything—all she had to live on"
(Mark 12:41-44 NIV).

There is no question that Scripture teaches us that giving demonstrates our obedience to God. Because we love him and have given 100 percent of ourselves to him, giving some of our money back to him so ministry can happen should be a piece of cake.

Remember, God is concerned with the attitude of your heart. If you don't give, or if you give with a bad attitude, God will know it and there will be no reward. The Bible says, *You must each decide in your heart how much to give. And don't give reluctantly or in response to pressure. "For God loves a person who gives cheerfully" (2 Corinthians 9:7 NLT).*

Whether you give 10 percent or 50 percent, the goal is to give with a cheerful heart, just like the poor widow who gave knowing that God would honor her and take care of her. If God honors cheerful givers, then we ought to make it a goal to become a hilarious giver.

BECOMING A GIVER

Begin Biblically
We've seen that God desires for us to give, not because we need to or because we want to receive his blessings, but because giving is a response of our love for him. We are also told to give with a cheerful heart. Jesus gives us another instruction for giving and that is to give without bringing attention to ourselves.

One of the teenagers in my youth group kind of spoke with a prideful attitude when he told me that he gives a weekly offering of $10. Why did he need to tell me? Giving is between him and God. I assume he was looking for a positive response from me. Instead I gave him a Scripture to look up and study—I wanted to help him learn so that he wouldn't lose his blessings from God by looking for human approval. Giving is between you and God and not anyone else.

Jesus tried to explain this in the Sermon on the Mount by telling people not to make noise with their trumpets when they gave but to give in private (see Matthew 6:1-4). It's very important to understand that giving should be between you and God.

> *"Give your gifts in private, and your Father, who sees everything, will reward you" (Matthew 6:4 NLT).*

Giving in secret is difficult because like the kid in my youth group, most of us want others to know how good or how righteous we are. But this defeats the purpose of giving! If we bring attention to ourselves then our hearts are not in the right place. I don't know about you, but I would rather receive my rewards from God than from the few people who may see me give or hear about my giving.

Find a Real-Life Example

To help you grow in this area of giving I want to challenge you to find someone who is a living, breathing example of a giver so you can understand more of the actions from this chapter. Learn from their giving attitude and then try to model yourself after him or her.

When I was first formulating my thoughts about giving, I used to watch my friend Alan. He was the most generous, selfless man I knew. He was always looking for ways to give, and his lifestyle simply became an unspoken challenge to those of us who spent time with him. Alan never gives glory to himself. He gives to God and others because he loves God and wants to honor God with his actions.

His daily prayer is: "Lord, show me how I can give of myself today to someone who needs your love." Accept the challenge to find an Alan for your life, a person you can watch and learn from. If you look hard enough you'll find someone like him.

Give Anonymously, Generously, Voluntarily, and Personally
There are many ways in which you can learn to give, but here are four specific ways to start being a giving person.

Anonymously: This is a great test of selfless giving. Those who possess a true giver's heart are embarrassed when their name is associated with their giving.

Generously: Giving liberally of your time, yourself, and your money communicates both a faith in God's provisions and an excitement for giving away the blessing God has given you.

Voluntarily: We have already mentioned the fact that giving needs to be done cheerfully, not because of arm-twisting or pressure or guilt.

Personally: It is important that we be personally involved in our giving. When our family gives to our church or to another organization, we pray for them and offer ourselves to them in whatever ways we can. This helps us to know where our money is going and it shows the church or organization that we are truly behind them.

This statement cannot be overemphasized: **Giving is our response to our love and obedience to God.** May your faith and your giving outgrow your dreams as you cheerfully become the giver that God desires for you to be.

LIVING LARGE TODAY

Use these questions for a time of reflection, as you write in your personal journal, or when you get together with your small group.

1. Why is it so difficult to not think about yourself first in most situations?

2. What do you think of the statement, "God is jealous over you"?

3. Why might God be more concerned about your attitude than the amount you give?

4. How would you currently rate yourself as a giver of your life, time, and finances? What might need to change within yourself to increase that rating?

> **Words can build up—and words can tear down. What words will you choose to come out of your mouth?**

5 ENCOURAGEMENT
The Life-Changing Power of Words

You've probably heard the old saying, "Sticks and stones will break my bones, but words will never hurt me." Well, it's just not true. As a matter of fact, it's a big, fat, hairy lie! Words hurt! Words are some of the most powerful weapons in our human arsenal, and they have the ability to change lives for the better or destroy them. Each of us holds the key to unlocking tremendous power through our word choices. In fact, the Bible says that the tongue is a small thing, but it can cause great damage or bring great joy (see James 3:5).

Every day you will find people around you who are dying for encouragement. You probably understand this because you're the same way. We all crave and need positive verbal strokes to keep us going since the majority of what we hear is negative. "Sit down!" "Shut up!" "Leave me alone!" "Can't you do anything right?" "Is that your face, or did your neck throw up?" "Why didn't you get that in on time?" Most of us would rather hear: "Hey, you look great today!" "You did a really good job on this!" "It's good to see you today!" "I really liked what you had to say in class today; I can tell you are a thinker."

Positive words have a way of making us feel warm inside, while negative words seem to freeze our insides with an uncomfortable and painful feeling.

The danger of being constantly exposed to negative input is that we can begin to believe these words. If people repeatedly tell you that you are ugly, you will probably begin to act and feel ugly. For example, it's common to hear prisoners talk about how negative words helped shape their performance in life. Many would say, "My dad always told me I'd end up behind bars, and I didn't let him down." These inmates lived out the negative words that they heard. This truth is tragic, yet it can bring us great joy to realize that what we say to others has the power to affect their lives in a positive way.

This chapter is written so that you might better understand the incredible force that your words can have and how you can better use this life-changing quality.

ENCOURAGEMENT...

...Can Make Others Feel Good About Themselves

When we receive a compliment, we feel good and think to ourselves, "Hey somebody noticed something good about me!" We feel as if someone cares enough not only to notice something nice, but also to mention it. You just feel different when people aim kind words your way.

God wants his people to feel special, because in his eyes, we are! Each of us was uniquely created by God while we were still in our mothers' wombs (Psalm 139:13-16). We were special enough for God to create this world and to send his Son to die for us.

When you decide to live large, be different, and shine bright, you will learn to make it a goal to pass along good words to help others feel good about themselves. Learn to give genuine compliments as a regular part of your day. Give it a try by challenging yourself to say something positive about every person you interact with. In return, you will feel great when their eyes light up in surprise and thankfulness.

The writer Mark Twain once said that he could live two months on one good compliment. So can your friends.

...Builds Confidence

Encouragement can be a strong force in building confidence. If someone affirms an ability you have, you will be more willing to put that ability to use. If you are constantly told that you are no good, you will be programmed to fail. (Remember the prisoner illustration?)

Four of the most important words in the English language are "I believe in you." My father and my youth pastor were two people who constantly said this powerful statement to me. When I was struggling to get through high school, college, and graduate school, they would tell me "I believe in you." Sometimes their support was all I needed to keep going.

Knowing that someone believes in you makes a world of difference. Every time I hear these words I am reminded of the positive support I received when I participated in sports and my parents cheered for me from the sidelines. I felt as though I could do anything because people were on my side believing in me. By the time I'd figured out that I wasn't going to become a professional athlete, their support had helped lead me down the path to what God had planned for my future.

There are people in your life who believe in you, but until they verbalize it you may feel like you are all alone. Who do you believe in but haven't actually told? They may be holding back and waiting for some belief and affirmation to help them move forward. The words they need to build their confidence may be "I believe in you." Try saying these words and watch the results.

...Brings Out the Best in People

I used to coach a soccer team of 6- and 7-year-olds. At our first practice I could see that our players didn't have much experience, so I decided that I would constantly encourage them so they would at least feel good about themselves when we lost our games. I showered them with positive words for not only their performance but for who they were as people.

By the time the season started we had 15 kids who really thought they were the best team in the league. They thought they were great, and that's exactly what they became. We never lost a game! To my surprise, I discovered that constant encouragement helped them discover their own talents and they played their very best. This is not just a great coaching tip—it's common sense for all of life.

When people feel better about themselves, they will look smarter, play harder, and perform better. People respond to their greatest potential when they feel good about themselves. Your words can make that all possible.

...Changes Lives

Jesus transformed the life of a big-mouthed fisherman when he changed Simon's name to Peter (John 1:42). Jesus didn't focus on Simon's weakness; instead he saw past all of Simon's sins and attitude problems and renamed him. Much to the surprise of Simon's friends, Jesus gave him the name Peter, which means rock. Later, in the book of Acts we see that the very foundation of the early church was built on the leadership of this rock named Peter. Jesus changed Peter's life by simply affirming him through a name change.

The power of words is so strong that even lives can be changed by the utterance of encouraging words. Your challenge is to realize the power of your words and affirm others wisely.

BECOMING AN ENCOURAGER

Realize That Affirming Others Doesn't Make You Look Bad

One of the most common reasons we fail to affirm others is our own low self-image. Simply put, many people are afraid that if they build someone else up, they will make themselves look bad. Or when we do choose to affirm someone, we do it in private so that others won't think the person we are complimenting is better than we are. To put it bluntly, this is a selfish attitude. We deprive others of love and positive words because we are afraid that we won't look as good in comparison. But the Bible tells us, *Love each other with genuine affection, and take delight in honoring each other (Romans 12:10 NLT).* This can be difficult to do, but if we can sincerely desire for others to look good regardless of how we look in comparison, we are well on our way to having a ministry of encouragement and shining bright. Read the following quote carefully, because it illustrates the importance of loving others:

"Most of us know our need to be loved, and try to seek the love that we need from others. If we seek the love which we need, we will never find it... we must face the fact that to be loved, we must become lovable... If a person, however, seeks not to receive love, but rather to give it, he will become lovable and he will most certainly be loved in the end." [1]

Search for the Positive

If you really make an effort and keep focused on encouraging others with your words, you will discover that every person has at least one quality or feature worthy of your notice and praise. The key to being a genuine encourager is speaking those words with sincerity. It's easy to sense if you are sincere in your affirmation. In fact, it is probably better to not say anything until you can actually speak good words with both truth and sincerity. You wouldn't want to say, "You played a great game!" if the person you are trying to affirm struck out three times and committed four errors. (This would be a good time for genuine comfort rather than insincere compliments.)

Also make sure in your search for the positive that what you consider to be an affirmation is also considered one by the recipient. For example, you wouldn't say, "You sure don't sweat much for a fat person" or "Your hair is a lot less greasy than usual." While those are funny comments, they aren't encouraging. Search for the truly positive.

Affirm Continually

Constantly affirm those with whom you come in contact. Place notes on your steering wheel, mirror, locker, and shoes that remind you to maintain an affirming attitude. If you can make it a habit, it can be one of the most amazing qualities that you will ever have in your life. Soon you will be known as the person who makes others feel special.

Use Encouragement as a Witness of God's Love

Encouragement can be a tremendous ministry to others and can have far greater implications than just making others feel better about themselves. You can actually begin to reveal to others the beautiful love God has placed in your heart. Others will begin to see that the Jesus you follow really makes a difference in all areas of your life—even your words.

Jesus says that what is in our heart will influence what we have to say. Your positive words will reflect the radiance of God's love that you received when you came into a relationship with him.

> *"For whatever is in your heart determines what you say. A good person produces good things from the treasury of a good heart, and an evil person produces evil things from the treasury of an evil heart" (Matthew 12:34b-35 NLT).*

You can also evaluate your encouragement as a gauge to where your heart is. Do positive or negative words come out of your mouth? If you find yourself feeling negative about others, your heart trouble may show up in your speech. This beautiful sentence says it all: "There is no human being who will not eventually respond to love if only he can realize that he is loved." [2]

Be praying that God would use your affirming words to reflect the source of where your encouragement originates. It is from God himself.

LIVING LARGE TODAY

Use these questions for a time of reflection, as you write in your personal journal, or when you get together with your small group.

1. What person in your life offers the most encouragement to you? What does this person say? How do you feel after receiving encouragement from this person?

2. What might your school or youth group look like if you became a stronger encourager? How might you help other people become stronger encouragers, too?

3. Identify one person in your life who needs some encouragement this week. How can you provide this encouragement, and when will do you do it? Who will hold you accountable and help you follow through on this commitment?

4. How can you turn encouragement into a regular habit in your life? What are some action steps you might take in the next week?

Being who you are isn't always easy. It's much easier to hide behind the masks we get so good at holding up to cover the real you. When you put the mask down and become transparent with who you are, you'll deepen your relationships.

6 TRANSPARENCY
An Honest Look at Genuine Relationships

If we truly desire to live large, be different, and shine bright, we need to acknowledge that most of us run around in constant fear—fear that we won't be accepted for who we are, fear that we will be laughed at, fear that we will be rejected. Because of these fears, we often put on false masks as if they were shields and pretend to be someone we really aren't, and when we enter the "battlefield" of relationships, we put our shields up so we won't get hurt.

In spite of our fears, we often have a deep, inner craving to tell someone who we really are—and what we really are like—without our masks. But this isn't easy to do. Just when we begin to be real, our fears creep in, and we quickly raise our shields of protection where it is safe and comfortable—and lonely.

Being transparent simply means being genuine or authentic. It means allowing others to see who you really are—faults and all. In relationships, transparency means opening up and letting others know the real you. Trust me…this is tough to do! It may be one of the most difficult actions discussed in this book. Most of us would much rather settle for the easy route of wearing a mask than risk being rejected. In this chapter we will look at the benefits of being transparent as well as some practical ways in which we can accomplish this goal within relationships.

BENEFITS OF BEING TRANSPARENT

It Strengthens Your Friendships

Being transparent will strengthen your friendships because you are letting someone else know you in a more intimate way. By sharing dreams, struggles, fears, and doubts with another person, you will develop a sense of bonding two hearts into a closer union.

When I was a junior in high school, I thought Jeff was my best friend because we did things together, laughed, talked about girls, and basically enjoyed each other's company. Our relationship changed one Friday night on the way to a high school football game, when I risked being rejected and was transparent with lack of knowledge about sexuality. I had pretended to understand some things people were always talking and joking about, but I really didn't understand. When I asked Jeff, he didn't treat me like I was an idiot for not knowing. We openly discussed my questions. After that evening Jeff and I began to talk about everything. He responded with being transparent about some of the things that were hiding below the surface of his life. We grew closer than we ever were before because we had begun to lower our shields and share our true selves. To this day Jeff and I share anything and everything, and I know that no matter what I say or do Jeff will still care about and accept me.

It Helps Other People

There are times when many of us feel that we are the only people in the world struggling with a certain problem or having a certain horrible thought. We tend to wallow in a pool of guilt or feel overly sorry for ourselves. By becoming transparent and allowing our friends to do the same thing, we learn that they have many of the same problems or thoughts as we do. We don't rejoice that other people have problems, but we do rejoice because we know that we aren't alone.

Transparency has changed my life! Right after I chose to follow Jesus, I began to hang around with my youth minister so I could learn more about my new faith. But the more time I spent with this godly man, the more I felt like I couldn't be a true man of God because I wasn't perfect like he was (or I assumed he was). He didn't seem to have any problems or hurts, while I was going through all of my weekly problems wondering why I was still struggling so much. He didn't do this intentionally, but I came to think that being a follower of Jesus meant being perfect, and I was ready to give it up because I knew I would never be perfect. After all, I saw "the real me" every day.

About this same time, a young, adult leader from the church moved into my family's home. His name was Mike and he was a great guy whom I respected and admired. Within a month of Mike's arrival into my family, his long-term girlfriend broke up with him, he had a major knee operation that put him on crutches for months, and he experienced family problems. Mike shared these struggles with me, and he told me about the hurt and pain that accompanied them. I lived through them with Mike as he cried out his questions and threw his crutches in disbelief and anger. Yet through it all, I saw that Mike continued to love and follow Jesus. Watching Mike work through his problems and challenges showed me that Christians weren't perfect, and his own messy, broken life gave me hope that I could be a follower of Jesus.

Mike's transparency changed my life. Being transparent is now a characteristic of my ministry because I know it helps others realize that they are not alone with their issues.

It Brings Healing
When a relationship is transparent, there will be times when you need to have the other person listen to all the struggles you are going through. There might even be times when you list all your sins and ask your friend to help you be accountable for being stronger in your faith.

In the book of James, there is an appeal for us to *confess your sins to each other and pray for each other so that you may be healed (James 5:16 NIV)*. James is promoting a transparency that gives us the freedom to discuss our weaknesses with another person. Notice that James writes "so that you may be healed." There is a real healing process that takes place when we confess to someone else areas in our lives that need help. The act of confession to another person (in addition to God who forgives us) helps us get these feelings out in the open where they can be seen in a different light and a new perspective. In addition, this accountability gives us greater reason to take action in resolving our sins.

BECOMING MORE TRANSPARENT IN YOUR RELATIONSHIPS

Be Selective

To start off, choose one friend who you feel you can trust. One person is easier to communicate with, and if you know this person cares about you then you are ready to experiment with being transparent and vulnerable. It would be unwise for you to try to let everyone in your group know your real self all at once. Not everyone is ready for your transparency. Some of your friends are in different places along their own personal journey, and you may experience some of the rejection that you fear. This does not mean that you want to give up your other friendships; simply start with the one person with whom you can learn to become more transparent.

Begin Slowly

A good rule to follow in this practice of becoming more transparent is to reveal a few honest thoughts or deep feelings at a time. Start slowly and evaluate the reaction of the other person. Does he or she really seem to care about you and your feelings? Can you trust this person or will he or she tell this to someone else? You may find that if you get hurt in your attempt to become more transparent, you will respond much more slowly, if at all, in your next attempt.

Encourage Mutual Transparency

The healthiest transparent relationships are the ones in which both people drop their masks. In fact, if only one of you is dropping their shield, I'd say that the relationship wasn't transparent at all. So if you find that the other person is doing all the listening, challenge him or her to slowly become more genuine with you. I am always more willing to risk letting another person know me better if that other person is also risking.

Be a Good Partner

Being a good partner in transparency is very important. Here are four solid rules to keep in mind when you are on the receiving end of a friend's transparency:

> **Don't give advice**—Put your personal opinions and your "genius" advice on hold, and simply listen. Too often we want to spout off our brilliant wisdom without really hearing. The other person needs an active listener. (We'll talk more about this in the chapter on Nonverbal Communication.)

> **Don't act shocked**—When someone reveals an intimate dream, fantasy, or thought, don't act as if you could never imagine such a thing. Simply accept and appreciate what they have to say before you respond.

> **Don't judge**—If we aren't careful, it's so easy to judge! Jesus tells us to remove the log out of our own eye before we look at the speck in another Christian's eye (see Matthew 7:15). If someone senses that they are being judged, they will be afraid of not being accepted and that will bring them back to their initial fear and their transparency will be quenched. Put yourself in their shoes.

Don't abuse confidence—You will become a real jerk if you go out and tell someone what was shared with you in a transparent and trusting manner. This is the easiest way to lose the special gift of having someone with whom you can be transparent.

God wants to bless us so that we might enjoy him and this earthly playground he gave us. Yet we so often find ways to take advantage of his blessings and mess things up. God gave us one another so that we might live out our lives in an intimate and personal manner. Being transparent within significant relationships is definitely risky, but it can prove to be one of the most rewarding experiences we can have. There is nothing like the wonderful feeling that comes when we openly give ourselves to another person and they accept us and give themselves back.

God loves us not for what we do, but for who we are. My prayer is that you would find someone in your life who also reflects this Christ-like attitude. It will change your relationship and ultimately change your life.

LIVING LARGE TODAY

Use these questions for a time of reflection, as you write in your personal journal, or when you get together with your small group.

1. What is the typical mask you wear to keep others from knowing the real you?

2. How have you seen a lack of transparency hurt or cheapen a relationship?

3. Do you have at least one safe person (friend, mentor, or small group leader) with whom you can confess your sins and find healing? If so, take time to thank that person for their role in your life. If not, how will you find one?

4. Have you hurt someone else by abusing the confidence they placed in you? If so, what might you need to do to make things right?

Some people are always talking but never really saying anything important. Others don't speak much but they say a lot with their body. What about you? What is your body saying?

7 NONVERBAL COMMUNICATION
When Actions Speak Louder Than Words

When I was in junior high, my afternoon routine was always the same. I would come home from school, walk in the door, and shout, "I'm home." Then I'd grab something to eat from the refrigerator (if I hadn't hit Taco Bell on the way home), move downstairs, and plant my body in front of the television until baseball practice.

Before long, my mom would make her way into the room and ask me the same question mothers have asked their child since time began: "How was your day, dear?" I would always reply, "Fine" with little or no emotion. Then she would persist and ask, "Well, what did you do today?" and I would give her the familiar answer. "Nothing," I'd say, continuing to stare at whatever was on the screen in front of me. My mom would finally let out a deep sigh, roll her eyes back, and—with the wonderfully sarcastic tone unique only to my mom—say, "I get so much pleasure out of our conversations."

One day, I remembered something a friend had told me he did with his mom, and I decided to give it a shot. I was going to give my mom her wish. I would tell her what I had done at school—exactly what I had done! When she asked me the usual question, I told her everything, starting with the moment I arrived at school.

"Well, Mom, when I got to school, I got off my bike, undid my combination lock (15-23-8, in case you ever need to open it yourself), and locked it up to Rick's bike. Then we both walked to my locker as I waved to Lindsey Cram, who was walking with Delia Baltiera—they are so cute! Then we went to Mr. Brazelton's P.E. class. But I didn't dress out because Bill Crane tried to light my shorts on fire. He's such a pyro."

I'm sure you get the picture. I did this with my mom for three straight days, and for some reason, the fourth day she didn't ask, "How was school?" In fact, she didn't even walk into the family room. I had talked her ear off. My friend's idea worked.

As I review this memory, I see that my mom and I communicated in several ways. First of all, I verbally communicated that I was home when I came through the door declaring my presence, then I communicated that I was hungry when I took food from the refrigerator, and I ultimately expressed my boredom by slouching in front of the television. My mom not only verbally communicated a question but also communicated a concern for me as a person. Through my non-enthusiastic response, I communicated a message that television was more important than talking with my mom. In her second question, Mom communicated that she really did want to talk to me. But finally she gave up and in her departing sarcastic response communicated her frustration for our lack of communication.

As you can see by this illustration, communication happens in a variety of ways, and we are capable of sending messages that we may not really want to give at all. Communication is so vital to living life fully and such an important skill, but it's also a very complicated skill. In fact, experts in communication point out that there are actually six messages that can come through when we communicate.

1. What you mean to say.
2. What you actually say.

3. What the other person hears.

4. What the other person thinks he/she hears.

5. What the other person says about what you said.

6. What you think the other person said about what you said.

Sounds confusing, doesn't it? And yet, communication is very important to who we are and what we are able to do as followers of Jesus. It is vital that we learn how to communicate so we can effectively care for others and share God's love with others.

I've called this chapter "Nonverbal Communication," but this doesn't mean that words aren't important (remember, the entire last chapter was on the power of our words). I just want to stress that "communication without the use of words" is a big deal. If you were to Google nonverbal communication and start poking around at the statistics you'd find some common reports that reveal that communication is 7 percent verbal (words only), 38 percent vocal (tones and inflections), and 55 percent facial (nonverbal). Again, this doesn't mean that words are meaningless in communication; they just aren't as significant to our message as we may believe.

The Bible has a good deal to teach us about the power of words and stresses the importance of controlling the tongue. But the truth is that what we do nonverbally often speaks louder than what we say. Isn't it true that it is easier to feel love than to hear about love?

> *"So now I am giving you a new commandment: Love each other. Just as I have loved you, you should love each other. Your love for one another will prove to the world that you are my disciples"* *(John 13:34-35 NLT).*

In this chapter we will look at two vital ways we can miss the mark in our attempt to communicate. Then, we'll think about three ways in which we can better understand and apply positive nonverbal communication in our own lives as we seek to live large, be different, and shine bright.

MISSING THE MARK IN COMMUNICATION

Listening but not Listening

When I was in college, one of my instructors told me that for about half (50 percent) of our day we listen, we hear half of what is said, we understand half of that, we believe half of that, and finally we remember half of what we believe. (For those not interested in doing the math, that means we remember only about 3 percent of what we hear!)

I share these statistics only to reinforce that even though we spend a great deal of our time "listening," we often don't hear much of what is being said. And if we don't hear what is being said, then we are not really communicating. Listening is a very important part of nonverbal communication. When we appear as if we are *not* listening, we communicate a message that the one who is talking isn't important to us.

I was at a convention recently when a man approached me and asked a question about my church. As I began to answer, I saw that he was looking right past me, nodding his head to appear as if he were paying attention. For all I know he may have heard every word I said, but because he wasn't looking at me, I felt (and feelings are very important in communication) as if he wasn't hearing me and really didn't care about my answer. It is awkward and embarrassing to feel like you are standing in a crowd talking to yourself.

What do you nonverbally communicate to your family and friends when they are talking to you? Do they feel like you are genuinely interested in what they are saying? Are you? If you value other people, you should become a master listener. Can you imagine Jesus, if he were here talking with us today, looking past us with a look that is the visual equivalent of someone impatiently drumming their fingers on a table in boredom? Don't you think Jesus would be hanging on our every word because he cares so deeply about us? Just like Jesus, we can communicate that we care when we actively listen.

Jumping to Conclusions

In all forms of communication, we have to interpret what we think the other person is trying to say. This can be difficult in nonverbal communication because in some ways, we have to read the other person's mind. Why? Because we can't hear what they are thinking. At least I can't.

The other night I was writing and was in deep concentration when my wife came home. I must have looked up at her over the computer (I don't remember doing it), and she later said my face had nonverbally communicated, "You told me you were going to be home at 6:30 and now it's 7:00; where have you been?" Although I hadn't said a word, she jumped to the conclusion that I was mad at her and went into the kitchen without making a sound. When I finished what I was writing, I began to wonder why she hadn't said anything to me when she got home and quickly jumped to the conclusion that she was disappointed with me because I had forgotten to take the meat out of the freezer like she had asked me to do. Fortunately, when we finally sat and talked, we realized that we perceived each other incorrectly, even though neither of us had said a word.

This sort of misunderstanding in communication happens all the time. Think about it. Someone gives us a dirty look, and we think they hate us when the look on their face was because their underwear was simply too tight or because they have gas. Or how about when we pull up next to another car and the driver smiles at us. We think they're flirting with us, but they are really laughing at how dumb we look. It is so easy to jump to conclusions when we don't take the time to make an accurate attempt to interpret nonverbal communication.

This puts us in a position to be embarrassed, wrong or—even worse—to get ourselves into relational trouble.

HITTING THE TARGET IN COMMUNICATION

Eye Contact

Eyes are such an active part of our communication process. If your eyes are actively looking at the person you are communicating with, they will feel that you are interested in what they are saying. Eye contact also communicates that the person you are with is important to you.

Some people have a hard time looking others in the eye. I used to have this problem. I overcame it by finding someone who is really good at making eye contact and studying her. I watched my friend Megan and the way she "talks" with her eyes. She makes me feel very comfortable because her expressive eyes show that she is concerned and interested in what I have to say. Megan makes me feel valued, and that encourages me to be open and honest in our relationship. The response she receives is amazing because her eyes communicate so much concern. If this is a problem for you, and you want to improve, remember: Practice makes perfect, so keep trying.

Body Language

Most of us are unaware of our own body language and how it communicates. But the fact is, we often communicate different feelings and attitudes that are interpreted in a variety of ways by other people. Most of us realize that this can be a challenge when we travel and experience other cultures, but it is even a problem right in our own little world called home.

If you and I were together, and you wanted to tell me some of your problems—or just wanted to talk—it would be important for me to remember not only to look at you, but also to be aware of the way I positioned my body.

For example, I would be rude to slouch in my chair turned away from you. Right?

A few years ago, I had the privilege of helping teach a college youth ministry class. In an early session, one student gave me this look that I interpreted as, "Who do you think you are to be teaching in this class?" Now that was discouraging! Another girl slouched so much in her seat that I could barely see her face, although I assumed that she had one. Half the time she slept in class, and she must have had a mouth and a nose to snore like that! Talk about nonverbal communication! She didn't want to be there, and she wasn't afraid of letting anybody know it!

Let your body language communicate that you want to be there and that you're interested in the person with whom you are communicating.

Appropriate Touch

God created us to be physical creatures, and touch is a very important aspect of our lives. From the very moment we are born, we require and desire touch and affection. I'll never forget holding my newborn children in my arms. They couldn't understand a word I said, but I know I communicated love by how gently I held them and by the way I caressed their tiny hands and faces. As we grow, we still need that same touch and caring. Touch is a vital form of communication: It communicates love, it calms our fears, it makes us feel comfortable, and it makes us feel wanted and special. If you can master the delicate art of appropriate touch, you will open up a whole new avenue of communication simply because you took the time to reach out.

Think about your own life for a minute. Can you remember a difficult time in your life when someone put their arm around you? Have you ever buried yourself in someone's chest and sobbed? Remember entering an uncomfortable situation for the first time and someone's handshake, hug, or high five helped ease the transition? Yeah! The right type of touch at the right time can make a big difference in someone's life.

Women are usually thought of as being more open to touching and being touched. Unfortunately, guys often grow up with the idea that it isn't good for boys to express emotion this way. I have a tragic memory of walking out of my kindergarten class innocently holding my friend's hand (I was only 5 years old.) My friend's father came rushing over to us with fear in his eyes, quickly broke apart our hands, and in a tense voice told me, "Don't ever hold hands again! I don't want anyone to think my son is gay!" I was devastated. I had no idea what the father meant, but that didn't really matter. All I knew was that there was obviously something terribly wrong about touching other guys (I already knew I would get cooties if I touched girls).

And yet, it is healthy to touch others with a hug or even with a handshake, but for some reason, this can still be a hard lesson to learn. A few years ago, I was speaking at a large high school camp. As I looked around the room, I realized that I had never seen a group of students who were more afraid of any type of physical contact. They each had what seemed like an invisible bubble around them, even as they sat side by side in the auditorium, so I decided to challenge them to use this great form of communication.

I told the guys that one way they can show that they care for each other (since guys often feel uncomfortable hugging) is by a playful punch in the arm. Maybe I should have chosen another phrase, because when I finished speaking, several of the guys got together, stood outside the door, and formed a punching line. As you can imagine, I was mauled when I walked out. By the time the camp ended, I was left with many bruises (one of which remains to this day), but I also left behind a group of students who finally realized the power of touch and the special message it can communicate when it is appropriate.

Each day, find ways to touch others: passing through a group and putting a hand on a shoulder as you go by, walking by a friend and lightly grabbing his or her arm, extending an arm to a friend, a handshake, a hug, a high five, or even a playful punch in the arm.

Now I am not challenging you to hang all over others or invade their privacy. There is still such a thing as respecting someone's personal space. But I do want you to understand that touching is needed and that it's a good way to communicate nonverbally.

As you finish this chapter, I pray that you'll reflect on the messages that you're sending with your body. You are communicating all the time, and it's easy to learn how to communicate love for others without even saying a word. Remember the challenge that Jesus gave us: "Others will know that you are my disciples (followers) by the way in which you show love for one another." I hope you better understand the importance of nonverbal communication and how it can increase your attempt to live large, be different, and shine bright. As St. Francis of Assisi said, "Preach God's love at all times, and when necessary use words."

LIVING LARGE TODAY

Use these questions for a time of reflection, as you write in your personal journal, or when you get together with your small group.

1. What do you think your nonverbal communication has been telling your parents lately?

2. When you listen, how do you know if you are really "listening"?

3. Why might eye contact be such a big deal in today's world?

4. What is a step you can take to become a person who uses touch in appropriate ways?

Meekness isn't weakness! Be strong by demonstrating this admirable quality. Details below.

8 MEEKNESS
A Gentle Strength

Before we discuss the concept of meekness, it is important to understand the true meaning of the word. My favorite definition of the word meek is the one used to describe a tamed stallion: a wild, powerful, and strong horse that has become gentle enough for a child to pet. It is a beautiful picture of strength under control. That's meekness—strength under control.

Definitions can also be helped by context, and the Bible often uses the word "meek" alongside the word "humility." Nowhere in Scripture does meekness have a negative meaning. On the contrary, the meek are mighty in God's eyes. (I read somewhere that they will inherit the earth!) For example, read this brief Bible passage discussing Moses: *Now the man Moses was very meek, more than all men that were on the face of the earth (Numbers 12:3 RSV).* Think about Moses' incredible life as a leader and all that he accomplished for God—and he was meek? Wow! Meekness is definitely not weakness. Again, it's strength under control.

Jesus is a perfect example of someone who displayed the quality of meekness in his life. His gentleness is seen when he gathered the children together and put them in his arms and blessed them (see Mark 10:13-16).

Another time, Jesus entered the Temple in Jerusalem and saw something similar to an unholy swap meet going on. There were people selling animals for sacrifices and money-changers charging outrageous rates of interest. Jesus' reaction was to chase the irreverent crowd out of the Temple with a whip. He angrily turned over their tables and yelled at them to not make his Father's house into a market (see John 2:13-16). That's a totally different response than the one he had when he gathered the children.

Both these examples provide extreme sides of Jesus' meekness. Yet they also help illustrate how diverse the personality of a meek person can be.

WHAT IS MEEKNESS?

It is not Weakness

Like many people, I associated meekness with weakness for many years. Maybe because they rhyme. Meek also rhymes with geek, which didn't improve the situation. But I thought that in order to be meek, I'd have to become a spineless person who didn't have any opinions, couldn't speak in front of others, and didn't have fun. Was I ever wrong! As I began to hang around other followers of Jesus, I began to observe some "meek" friends and watch them. I also spent more time studying Scripture and learning from the life of Christ. Jesus spoke his message in front of thousands, had the power and authority to heal people, raised others from the dead, and was a leader of many. Yet the Bible said that he was meek. That really made me think.

Sensitivity is another form of meekness that is often viewed as weakness. Young men are encouraged to not express any emotion or feelings. When they begin to cry they are told, "Big boys don't cry, so stop crying." As a result, many guys grow up having a hard time expressing their feelings. They repress tears because "big boys don't cry." They may even believe that it's not manly to show empathy, pity, and concern.

What a typically macho, insensitive male doesn't realize is that most women prefer being around a sensitive man more than an inflated, self-promoting man. Most women relate better (and feel that they are treated better) by sensitive guys. It makes perfect sense, because sensitive people tend to be more affirming and have a genuine Christ-like concern for others.

It is Humility

Being humble means being able to put other people before yourself. Someone who is humble enjoys being a "behind-the-scenes" person. They don't crave the spotlight or excessive attention. A humble person receives a true sense of joy from seeing other people receive attention. As a matter of fact, a truly humble person will help others receive attention without taking any credit. That is a rare but attractive quality!

I am often impressed when I hear professional athletes take the spotlight off themselves and give other players—or their entire team—credit for their performance. That is humility in action.

Jesus used the example of a small child to illustrate true humility because children have pure hearts.

"Unless you change and become like little children, you will never enter the kingdom of heaven. Therefore, whoever humbles himself like this child is the greatest in the kingdom of heaven" (Matthew 18:3-4 NIV).

It is Servanthood

Servanthood is another form of humility, and it's a quality that is so important to develop as a follower of Jesus. Jesus said that he came not to be served but to serve and to give his life as a ransom for many (see Mark 10:45). Jesus is the ultimate example of servanthood, not only for the many acts of service that he cheerfully completed, but also for giving his entire life so that we might live eternally.

You can bet that people who possess the quality of meekness are among the greatest of servants.

It is Gentleness

People who are meek often have a gentle, quiet spirit that can work against them in this noisy, "me-first" world. They aren't loud, obnoxious, or rude. They have a real peace about them, and there is real beauty in this peaceful calmness. Their actions are gentle and caring. They don't force their opinion on others but are usually asked their opinion because they speak with such wisdom.

Christ's gentleness is seen in his lifestyle. The Apostle Paul used Jesus as an example when he said, *By the meekness and gentleness of Christ, I appeal to you (2 Corinthians 10:1 NIV).* As you attempt to live large, be different, and shine bright, may your gentleness be a reflection of your life.

MAKING MEEKNESS WORK

Be Slow to Speak

This is a challenging action for me. I have strong opinions about things and want to make sure that others hear them. I usually lean forward in my seat so that I can drop my pearls of wisdom into the conversation. But truly meek people are in control of their tongues during conversations. They think before they speak so that their words will have meaning and impact. Meek people are usually good listeners (see chapter 7 on Nonverbal Communication) who are more interested in the person than in their content.

> *My dear brothers, take note of this: Everyone should be quick to listen, slow to speak and slow to become angry (James 1:19 NIV).*

The next time you are involved in a conversation with a group, try this out. Sit back and observe the other people as you listen to the dialogue. Pray for the people that are speaking, and even ask God to guide your words so that if and when you do speak, it will be with wisdom.

Put Others Before Yourself
Putting others first sounds like such a simple rule, yet (like so many other simple rules) it is very difficult to put into practice. Our meek friends have the heart of servants and seem to be able to put others before themselves very naturally. This is an attitude Jesus tried to teach his disciples before he returned to his Father.

In the Gospel of John there is a beautiful description of Christ at the Last Supper, as he walked up to each of his disciples and washed their feet. Although some of them were reluctant for him do this, Jesus explained why he humbled himself in such a manner.

"And since I, your Lord and Teacher, have washed your feet, you ought to wash each other's feet. I have given you an example to follow. Do as I have done to you" (John 13:14-15 NLT).

Jesus showed he was a servant by putting others first. Developing a servant's heart is a response to the world because of our faith in Christ. We don't serve seeking a reward or to be admired. We serve simply because we love Jesus and because we see Christ's example and want to imitate him. We are never more like Jesus than when we serve.

Meek people serve in small ways as well as large. They are often the first ones to volunteer when asked. They don't race to be first in line, they sit in the back seat of the car, they pick up litter that you and I walk over, they bring in the neighbor's trash cans, they give up their seats so another can have one, and they wait in line to buy tickets for everyone else while their friends goof around. These aren't the only actions of a servant, but they can give you a good idea of some of the smaller ways in which meek people serve. But here's the important lesson: The one thing that each of these small ways of serving has in common is that you and I can easily do them. If you're like me, you need to start with the small acts of servanthood and slowly work into making serving part of your lifestyle. By doing this we will be strengthened in our pursuit of meekness.

Recognize God's Greatness
The Bible speaks of fearing God. This doesn't mean that we should be afraid of him but that we should be in *awe* of him. When we understand how awesome God is we will be able to see ourselves in a better perspective.

One of the things that can keep us from being meek is having an overly inflated idea of who we are. But the fact is, we are nothing compared to God. We need to adopt the attitude of David the psalmist, who praised God for his greatness and majesty and at the same time considered himself a worm (see Psalm 22). Fortunately, God doesn't treat us like worms even though that's what we are in comparison to him.

A meek person realizes his or her true status before God. It is only because of God's grace (undeserved favor he grants us) that we have been given life with him. When we choose to follow Jesus, we are new creations. The old creation no longer exists, because God is in the process of making you (and me) into the image of Christ (see 2 Corinthians 5:13-20). When you really understand this you will realize that the beautiful, sensitive, humble quality of meekness comes from knowing that God has the power and love to make you his new creation.

LIVING LARGE TODAY

Use these questions for a time of reflection, as you write in your personal journal, or when you get together with your small group.

1. How would you have described the word "meek" before reading their chapter? How might your definition have changed now that you've finished reading?

2. Why do you think everything inside of us fights humility?

3. If you try being slow to speak this week, what do you think might happen?

4. Where do you see examples of servanthood in your life today?

No one enjoys being left out of a crowd, and everyone enjoys being invited to something. What might it look like if your life became more inviting and less exclusive?

9 CLIQUES
Creating a Welcoming Environment

Many people believe that cliques exist only in the church, but the truth is that cliques exist everywhere. There will always be those on the outside and those on the inside. But it doesn't have to be that way! If you could learn to become a clique buster as a teenager, you would develop a much needed and valued skill. Even though cliques begin in preschool and continue into adulthood, you can help change that reality—one clique at a time!

A clique can be defined as a "closed" group—in other words, a group that isn't interested in including new people. You can probably think of examples of cliques in your neighborhood, church, school, and work place. You may even be part of one yourself! Before you get defensive, I know that becoming part of a clique may happen to us unconsciously. In other words, it may simply be the natural outgrowth of long-term friendships—and that can be a positive statement about good friendships. But whether it happened accidentally or on purpose, once we are conscious that we are part of a clique or a group that is excluding others, if we're really going to learn to live large, be different, and shine bright we need to learn how to respond appropriately.

Many many years ago I heard the following song lyrics and it caught my attention and caused me to want to do something about the cliques that

I was around. Read these words carefully, and I pray that you might be sensitized to those waiting outside your group.

Elaine lives on the bad side of town
Nothing goes on there, it only goes down
Her family is a sad situation
and she's the victim of their frustration
Down the street at the church it's a different world
Wednesday night and Sunday
The Christians there could really help that girl
If only they would say

(Chorus)
COME ON ELAINE COME ON ELAINE
COME ON ELAINE Let's get together
COME ON ELAINE Oh Elaine
COME ON ELAINE
We'll try to make it better (for you)

At her school nobody knows she's there
Except to laugh at how she does her hair
She ain't got money for the Sassoon [fancy] jeans
She don't know how to play the video machines

Well at the church there's a girl who could reach her
But it's kinda out of her way
Her choice of friends is her finest feature
And she's too cool to say

(Chorus)

We'll try to make it better for you
You need to know somebody cares for you
Someone to help with what you're going through
And share the love of Jesus with you.[3]

Do you know anyone like Elaine? Do you ever notice those on the "outside"? Regardless if you know them or not, they're there. What are you going to do about them?

CLIQUES DAMAGE...

...A Welcoming Youth Group

When someone new walks into your youth group, do they feel loved and accepted? They won't stay or get involved if they don't feel accepted.

I can think of very few times when someone new to my youth group has introduced himself to me and asked how he could get involved. Usually, teenagers will visit and wait to see if they are greeted and accepted. If the group is friendly, it is easier for them to get involved. But if they don't feel welcome, they lose interest and leave—often with bad feelings—and often never to return. Your group may be composed of really great people, but if they are not friendly to visitors, they aren't going to earn (or deserve) a good reputation.

...Potential Friendships

Growing up, I was involved with a group of friends from my church who became very close. Many of them would eventually work in full-time ministry; this was one of the many things we shared in addition to enjoying each other's company.

We referred to ourselves as the "gang." (I know, it sounds tough, doesn't it? No!). As time went by and we got older, we began to spread out into various cities, we started calling ourselves the "Orange Gang" because we all came from the city of Orange, California.

But something very interesting happened when some of us began to get involved in serious relationships outside of the Orange Gang. Our tight little group had built such a strong bond of friendship that it was difficult for our new girlfriends and boyfriends to feel comfortable when the gang was together. I was totally unaware of this until I met my future wife, and she began to share her feelings with me about my friends from an "outsider's" perspective. Soon, I learned that other outsiders had similar feelings. Honestly, the Orange Gang never intended to be a clique, we were just so comfortable with each other that we didn't make a big enough effort to welcome newcomers, even those we really liked!

No group, not even a group of potential ministers, is immune to becoming a clique.

Here's the bottom line: If someone doesn't feel accepted, they are well on their way to feeling alienated. Those of us who have experienced alienation know that to feel unwanted is a horrible feeling. There isn't much of a gray area in this situation. Even if we understand that God loves us unconditionally, we still have a hard time when we aren't allowed to become part of a group we desire to join. Since Jesus was all about "outsiders" those of us who are followers of Jesus should take on his values. The church should be the last place on the face of the earth where people would feel unwanted and un-welcomed, yet this type of alienation takes place in youth groups (and adult congregations!) everywhere.

Acceptance of others should be a byproduct of—and a response to—the obedience and love that you have for God.

> *I pray that your love will overflow more and more, and that you will keep on growing in knowledge and understanding (Philippians 1:9 NLT).*

Paul's words should challenge Christ-followers and youth groups to overflow with love and open up to others.

...God's Plan for Reaching Others
One of the ways in which God has chosen to reach those that don't know Jesus is through his Church (his body of believers). But when the

church doesn't accept outsiders, it really is nothing more than a Christian club. And if God wanted us to have a Christian club he would have already taken us up to heaven so we could be exclusively with other believers. Yet God chose differently. He wants his Church (you and me) to welcome those who don't know him, and he left that largely up to us.

Throughout the New Testament there is an appeal to reach those outside the church with the reality that Jesus died for the sins of all humanity. If we take God's Word seriously, then we need to open our lives, our churches, and our youth groups to others. We can't afford to hide in our cliques if we are to effectively live out God's plan.

BECOMING A "CLIQUE BUSTER"

Start With Another Person

Once you have decided that you need to make some changes (and I'm certain you will to some degree after reading and reflecting on this chapter), it is important for you to help someone else understand the important action of breaking up cliques. Explain and discuss how dangerous cliques can become, and ask if he or she is willing to help you become a clique buster. Why? It is easier to do with another person helping and supporting you.

Develop a strategy. Decide who you should talk to and what cliques are most corruptive. Take each person in the group aside individually, and ask them for their help and understanding as you work to open it up to others and reflect the love of Jesus.

Bring People Into Your Group

Many of us learn by example, so this may be a time when you need to set the standard for your group. In a loving manner (as opposed to being cocky or pious), begin reaching out to new people. Actively watch out for them at the beginning of your meetings (they're usually the ones alone and looking uncomfortable), greet them, and invite them to sit with you and become a part of your group. Spend time with them, and make it a point to try to incorporate them into the life of your friends. In a very real sense you can become a minister to outsiders. This doesn't mean that you give up all your old friends, but that you are open to adding to the group. Remember, even your oldest friends were strangers when you first met them.

As other cliques are exposed to what you are trying to do, they may catch the vision and want to become involved in clique busting too. You might begin a revolution within your youth ministry that can spread like a virus within your entire church.

Pray for Sensitivity

This is a very important step in becoming a clique buster, and (like many of my life lessons) I learned this from my wife. Before every program, meeting, or party she prays that God will make her sensitive to the needs of those with whom she will come in contact. It's really amazing what happens—most of the time God directs her to people who are on the outside of the group and are feeling uncomfortable. She immediately becomes light in the midst of darkness.

Try this experiment this week: Every time you enter a situation where there may be outsiders, ask God to help you find people who might need a friendly greeting or a connection. Beg for God to give you eyes to see what you normally don't see. You'll probably be amazed at what happens.

If after reading this chapter you don't think that there is a need in your group for a clique buster, you are either involved in a very unusually friendly group of people who are sensitive to God's Spirit and leading (which would be great) or you aren't looking hard enough. Consider this truth: People will judge Christianity, Jesus, and those who follow Jesus by the way they are treated when they enter your environment. You're called to be something more than a clique—you're called to be different. You can do it!

LIVING LARGE TODAY

Use these questions for a time of reflection, as you write in your personal journal, or when you get together with your small group.

1. When was the last time you were left out of a group? How did it feel?

2. What actions might you be able to take to help others in your group understand the negative power of cliques?

3. What are going to be your immediate steps to change how you look for outsiders?

4. Respond to this quote: "Cliques are nothing more than fellowship gone ugly!"

You've heard it before: Second place is the first loser. Drink Gatorade and be a winner. Live strong. So, are you a winner or a loser? Actually, it doesn't matter—here's how to really win.

10 COMPETITION
Do You Always
Have to Win?

I love to watch professional athletes give their all to be the best and win. Talk about living large! For them, winning is everything! For the professional, it makes perfect sense, because the better they play (and the more they win), the better their prospects will be when their agent negotiates their next contract. Basically it comes down to this: For a professional athlete, the better they play, the more money they will make.

Those of us who aren't professional athletes don't have this type of performance pressure—or we shouldn't. But whether we play the piano, paint murals, or play basketball, we often find ourselves in competition with others. In fact, most of us don't even need a human opponent, for we even compete against ourselves (to achieve a "personal best" score or time) and against a standard, such as when we take a test.

Just this morning I was wondering if writing a chapter on competition would really be helpful and make it onto the list of the top 12 issues. Then, at 3:00 this afternoon, my church high school group got together to play street hockey—and they just about killed each other. I broke up at least three fights and took stick whips to my shins until I could barely walk. There was one argument about whether one of the goals was a clean goal or a ricochet. Who cares? Why argue? It was still a goal.

One of the teenagers summed up the feeling of the day when he said, "We are not going to quit until we win!" When the painful marathon finally ended, I hobbled back to my office, fully convinced that a chapter on a healthy view of competition was definitely needed—at least in my own youth ministry!

In this chapter we will take a look at a few attitudes that can be dangerous to your spiritual growth if not handled properly. Then we will look at some realistic ways in which everyone (competitive or not) can develop positive attitudes that will help us in our goal to live large, be different, and shine bright.

COMPETITIVE ATTITUDES

The "Do Anything to Win" Attitude

Some people place such a big emphasis on winning that they will do whatever it may take to win, even if it is going to hurt others. I remember hearing one story in particular. Several years ago, a woman named Rosie Ruiz crossed the finish line in the Boston Marathon with a world record time, only to be later disqualified when it was proved she didn't run the entire race. She had jumped into the pack of runners near the end of the 26-mile run. Unfortunately, before she was disqualified, she stole all the media attention from the real female winner, whose name is rarely remembered today (it's Jackie Gareau in case you wondered—I had to look it up). Was winning really that important to Rosie? Apparently it was.

I remember a story of a Soap Box Derby champion who was disqualified because he used a specially designed, illegal magnet to help him get down the hill faster. Why? To win, of course. Some people will always sacrifice their integrity (remember chapter 1) for the short-lived pleasure of winning.

These days, the major buzz kill among professional athletes is performance-enhancing drugs, as players from the NFL, Major League Baseball, and other sports seek to find any edge they can to beat out an opponent to keep in the limelight, even if it is illegal. Yes, Mark McGwire broke Hank Aaron's home run record, but he later admitted to using steroids. A tarnished record. In the white-hot spotlight of big-money sports, many athletes don't understand this biblical truth: *And athletes cannot win the prize unless they follow the rules (2 Timothy 2:5 NLT).*

But as the athletes we admire struggle with this issue of competition, so do the "normal" people like you and me. We need to see and help others understand that winning isn't everything. The old saying, "Winning isn't everything, it's how you play the game" seems outdated because all too often there are plenty of people and teams who will do anything to win. I know parents who will pressure their young children to win. It's not just the professionals who struggle.

When my younger sister was 10 years old, she decided to play soccer for the first time. She was placed in a league filled for girls aged 11 to 13, but turned out to be the only girl on the team who was not only the youngest, but had never played before. Because of her inexperience, she didn't get to play very much, and when the coach did play her, he hid her in a position of little action.

During one particularly important and close game, the time came for Stacy to play. Just before she went in, one of the parents said, "Now that she's going in, we're going to lose for sure."

Everyone heard this stupid comment, and my sister went onto the field with her ears ringing with those insensitive words and her fragile confidence destroyed. She fell apart and her team lost the game. Of course, because of the woman's comment, my sister believed it was all her fault and didn't even want to finish playing out the season. She never played soccer again, in large part because of the painful experience created by one parent's overwhelming desire to win.

Let's be honest, winning is great! It's fun. It's exciting to win and it's a lot more enjoyable than losing. But winning shouldn't be so important that you compromise your integrity to achieve it. In fact, when you make winning a supreme goal it can be destructive to your personality. You will also set yourself up for failure because no one wins at everything, and it will be to your advantage to realize now that you can't and won't win at everything in life. Plus, winning without integrity isn't winning at all.

As you develop into a teenager who lives large, is different, and shines bright, it is very important to learn how to go through life without comparing yourself to others. When you compare, you will always lose. If you look far enough, there will always be someone who is able to talk better, look better, or in some other way outdo you. And if you compare and find yourself being better, you can become prideful and that's definitely a loser attitude in God's eyes (he hates pride).

The "I Hate to Lose" Attitude

It makes sense that people who will do anything to win usually have a hard time losing. Their competitive nature is so intense that when they lose (and they eventually do), they hate it so much that it impacts their attitude and ultimately their life.

Recently, one of our high school Bible study groups challenged another to a football game. It was wild! Each group wanted to win so badly that they brought in varsity football players from their schools to help. They wanted to stack the deck, load the team, and increase their chances to win. (I later found it interesting that they wouldn't invite these guys to church but they'd invite them to help them win a game. Hmmm, maybe I need to move from writing a chapter to teaching this material to the teenagers in my ministry.)

After the game was over we were walking off the field and one of the students said to me, "I hate to lose."

I quickly responded, "You didn't lose, you tied."

He answered, "I was always taught that if you tied, you might as well consider it a loss."

How unfortunate that this young man left a fun day of playing with that negative attitude! By placing so much emphasis on winning, he wasn't able to enjoy a really competitive and exciting, evenly matched contest. I wish he would have walked away thinking, "Hey that was a tough but fun game."

Those who hate to lose are usually the same ones who are considered poor sports and who do the most judging and complaining. I played organized, competitive sports for 12 years. I realized early that it is fun to win, especially when there is something at stake. But to take competition so seriously that you are significantly bothered by losing can be destructive to both your personality and your relationships. If that describes you, something needs to change.

If your self-image is based largely on whether you win or lose, you will probably find yourself being incredibly competitive. When I was in high school, I may have been the most competitive person around. I would do anything to win, and I did. When I lost I wasn't fun to be around. Basically when it came to competition, I was an idiot.

One Sunday night, my youth group was playing Ultimate Frisbee in the church parking lot. I was being my usual competitive self, knocking people around and doing whatever it would take to win when my youth pastor pulled me aside.

He said, "You are a good athlete, but you will never be an effective minister for Jesus if you continue to act the way you do during competition. You are turning people off."

That night I went home and reflected on what he had said. I realized that one of the reasons I wanted to win so badly was because winning was good for my ego. It feels good to be on the winning side. It's nice to be chosen to play on the winning team. It feels good to receive compliments for playing well. As I reflected, I realized that all of my reasons for wanting to win were selfish—they were all about me. It was then that I knew I had to change.

Years later, I now understand what my youth pastor was trying to tell me. By focusing on myself and trying so hard to be a winner, I was more interested in me than I was in the well-being and success of others. To be an effective minister of Jesus (which is what Christians are called to be) we must learn to take our eyes off ourselves and focus them on the Lord and on others.

HAVING THE PROPER ATTITUDE OF COMPETITION

Develop an Attitude of Fun

Learning to have fun while competing has nothing to do with talent. You can be athletically challenged, musically goofy, and academically inept and still learn to have a winning attitude. A winning attitude is one that views the competitions that life brings as fun. This attitude is an expression of thankfulness for the talents and abilities that God has given you.

I love the phrase "ARE WE HAVING FUN YET?" You may be losing a football game by 100 points and still be having fun. You may have come in fifth place in a speech contest and still have had fun because of the people you met and the opportunity you had to share your speech. If you can come to learn that fun doesn't always have to be connected to winning you will come out ahead.

Your winning attitude can turn around an entire team. Continually remind yourself, your friends, and your team that you are having a good time while competing (with phrases like "Isn't this fun?"). Life is so different when it's lived as though we are acknowledging all the great things that God put on this earth. God has given us an incredible playground called "earth" for us to live on and enjoy as we worship and serve him. Develop that mindset and you'll really become a winner!

Focus on Doing Your Best

When you are competing, do your best. God has given you some specific talents. Use them. Develop an attitude of wanting to do the very best you can with what God has given you. The Apostle Paul told the church in Corinth, *So whether you eat or drink, or whatever you do, do it all for the glory of God (1 Corinthians 10:31 NLT).* Giving your very best is one way of giving glory to God for what he has given you. Obviously doing your best to the glory of God does not involve fostering an overly competitive attitude, hurting others, or drawing attention to yourself.

Have you ever heard a Christian performer make a statement after a great performance that sounds something like this: "Well, it wasn't me— it was God." This has always struck me as unusual and even kind of funny. I've always wanted to say to that person, "I could have sworn that was you and not God because I saw your mouth move when you sang." I'm sure their heart is right and I'd bet that what they're really trying to say is that God has given them the power and the abilities to perform. It was their performance but it was God who graciously gave them the ability to do what they did. You can do that too! Do what you do to the best of your God-given ability and do everything to the glory of God.

> *And whatever you do, whether in word or deed, do it all in the name of the Lord Jesus, giving thanks to God the Father through him (Colossians 3:17 NIV).*

Realize That God's Acceptance is for Winners and Losers

It is very important to understand that God loves you not for what you do or how good you are but for simply being his creation. God loves us so much that he gave his only son to die for us so that we might live eternally if we believe in him (see John 3:16).

It's really hard to understand why God loves us so much even though we mess up and are disobedient to his ways. But the important and saving fact is that God does love you—even in your messiness.

> *But God showed his great love for us by sending Christ to die for us while we were still sinners (Romans 5:8 NLT).*

You may be the last person picked on every team you ever try out for, but to God, you're Number One. God doesn't treat you any differently if you lose the big game or make a mistake on your solo performance. And he won't reward you any differently if you spend the rest of your competitive years on a losing team. He will still pick you for his All-Star Team.

If you understand this truth about God then you can do your very best for him and not be so concerned about every score of every game. When you begin to embody some of the positive aspects of competition you can learn to enjoy losing as much as winning just because you'll know God has you on his team.

LIVING LARGE TODAY

Use these questions for a time of reflection, as you write in your personal journal, or when you get together with your small group.

1. Think of some professional athletes who have sacrificed their integrity to win. Do you think it was worth it once they were exposed as cheats?

2. When you play, do you play to win, or play to have fun? Which is better/right?

3. Have you ever been picked last? How did it feel?

4. What do you think it might take for you to "win" at life? What are you doing to get there?

Have you ever laughed so hard that milk came out of your nose? Laughter is a big deal. A good sense of humor not only makes you more attractive, but it helps others feel more comfortable. There's a lot of crazy stuff in our world, and everyone could use a little more laughter and joy.

11 LAUGHTER
Adding Joy to Your Life

This will be a fun chapter to read! It's not a funny chapter (at least not intentionally), but it is one that will give you something fun and exciting to think about. My purpose isn't to make you a comedian, but to present just a few of the many reasons why it is good for you to laugh. Then we'll share a few ideas on how you might develop a better sense of humor.

There isn't a great deal about laughter in the Bible. There aren't verses that say, "Thou shalt laugh." We don't have any accounts of Jesus cracking jokes to his disciples. Nor do we have record of Jesus saying, "I want to teach you how to make others laugh so that when I am gone there will still be laughter in the world." But just because Jesus didn't leave specific instructions on how to giggle, snicker, chortle, or guffaw doesn't mean that he didn't laugh.

You may be thinking, how can laughter and God go together? The Jesus that we've seen depicted in religious films is always so serious—he usually speaks in an intense, deep voice and appears angelic and decidedly non-human. But because Jesus was 100 percent human (born in a stable, remember?) and he hung out with a bunch of guys, it's reasonable to assume he laughed. Think of the people and the situations that surrounded him. Imagine the look on the face of the guy who was carrying the jug of water when Jesus turned it into wine (see John 2). I can see a classic double take there. Maybe even a spit take if the guy took a drink of what he thought was water! Or the reaction of the crowd when four guys had the nerve to lower their crippled buddy through a hole (that they created) in the roof of the house where Jesus was preaching (see Mark 2). Can't you just see Jesus sitting there with roof tiles falling all around him?

There are several other biblical events that are just laugh-out-loud funny if we only imagine our reaction to them as if they were happening today. But even though the Bible says little directly about laughter, it does cover the topic indirectly in at least one verse.

> *A cheerful heart is good medicine, but a broken spirit saps a person's strength (Proverbs 17:22 NLT).*

Another word found frequently in the Bible with a similar meaning to "cheerful" is the word "joy." The Bible has numerous verses that speak of joy and gladness in the same thought.

When I think of the word joy, it brings to mind feelings of happiness, good times, and laughter. If joy is present in your life, it is usually accompanied by smiles and the ability to laugh. It is much easier to be a person who uses and appreciates laughter when there is joy in your life.

Unless you enjoy being unhappy, laughter should come easily to you. But if you're one of "those" people, at least try reading the rest of this chapter with an open mind and a grin on your face.

WHY IT'S GOOD TO LAUGH

Laughter Helps Bring Joy Into the Lives of Others

I love to be with friends, laughing and having a good time. People who love to laugh are some of the most joyful people I know.

When I was in college, I used to look forward to Thursday nights with great anticipation. That was the night I would go to a restaurant, meet a friend or two, drink gallons of iced tea, and talk and laugh until the early hours of the morning. The reason that I loved this time so much is that it brought joy into my life during a particularly stressful time. Many days during college it seemed like I moved from pressure to stress to rush to study to exhaustion. I really needed a super-sized order of the joy that laughter brought me.

There are many people in the world today who seem "happy" being unhappy. They seek out the bad and ignore all the good. Instead of having a joyful heart, they have a depressed one. I see people like this all the time. Some of them are in my youth group. But laughter is an amazing gift and can ignite a spark of joy to even a depressed heart.

Laughter Makes People Feel Comfortable

There are times when we are in a tense situation, and all of a sudden, laughter breaks the tension. Have you ever had that happen to you? We feel so much better! This happens to me when I walk in the dark. I'm afraid of the dark (don't act shocked and surprised, you probably are too). When I enter a dark room, I want to get the lights on right away. In the meantime I use laughter as my flashlight. As I'm searching for the light switch and feeling tense, I force myself to laugh so I won't be so scared. As odd as it sounds, it really works!

There may be times when a person entering your youth group or classroom for the first time is incredibly uncomfortable. This is probably a great time to lighten the tension with some laughter. Maybe you tell them, "It's good to meet you. This room may smell like a locker room, but it's really a great place to be" or "Oh, you go to University High School, that's great. We've been trying to upgrade the people in this group for some time now." As long as you do not use put-downs or make a newcomer the subject of the joke, light humor can make the new person feel comfortable and can help make a good first impression.

Of course, as with any rule, there are some exceptions! Recently, my wife and I were going to the house of one of my old high school friends for a party, a sort of reunion. She knew very few people and naturally felt uncomfortable. Another old friend of mine met us at the door and immediately launched into a rude, gross joke. He thought it was really funny, but my wife felt uncomfortable, which made him uneasy, and the remainder of the evening had an awkward feel.

It helps to use tasteful and affirming humor when you try to make others feel comfortable.

Laughter Can Make People Feel Better Physically

The value of laughter goes beyond good feelings. In fact, scientific studies have been published indicating that laughing can actually be good for your health. There's an old story of a doctor who said, "If you can't take a joke, then you'll have to take medicine."

Several years ago, a man named Norman Cousins wrote a bestselling book, *Anatomy of an Illness*, which told how laughter cured him of an incurable form of spinal arthritis. It's a remarkable, true story!

Another way laughter helps us feel healthier is when it provides a release from tension. In his book *Laughter and Health*, Dr. James J. Walsh says that laughter provides a much needed massaging of the lungs, heart, liver, pancreas, and intestines. Who am I to argue with a doctor?

We're not suggesting that you watch the newest cable comedies or read your friend's crazy blog posts or overdose on YouTube videos instead of going to the doctor, but it is good to know that laughter can have a positive effect on your body.

Laughter Helps Others Be More Receptive

When I speak at a camp or to a school group, I'll usually begin with a funny story that I know will relate to my topic and make my audience laugh. Laughter helps in communication. When I get up to speak to teenagers I know what they're thinking—consciously or subconsciously:

"Why should I listen to this balding, old guy?" But as soon as there's a little laughter in the room, their body language changes and all of a sudden they treat me like maybe this old guy has something to say.

Give this a shot. The next time you're sitting and listening to someone speak, study the audience's reaction to a crazy video, or watch when someone tells a funny story or a good joke. The energy in the room will triple, and the audience will come alive. It will be as if someone had wired their chairs with an electric charge while pumping oxygen into the room.

In the book *Secrets of Successful Humor*, the authors give seven reasons why laughter works with both individuals and audiences:

1. It is one of the most effective forms of emotional communication.
2. It can dissolve tension in people to whom you are relating and can help them relax.
3. It can help you gain and keep your listeners' attention.
4. It can increase your credibility (earning the right to be heard) and help you come across as a real person.
5. It can help overcome resistance to points you are trying to make.
6. It can provide needed breaks in a conversation or speech.
7. It can help drive home a point.

These points are important to keep in mind when you are speaking to others. If we take the importance of sharing the good news of Jesus Christ seriously, we need to be the best possible communicators that we can be. I'm not suggesting that you need to become a great public speaker, but I am saying that we need to know how humor can help us better communicate the life-changing message of Jesus.

Along with a better understanding of what laughter can do for us, one of the ways to live large, be different, and shine bright is to develop a better sense of humor.

Laughter Doesn't Expose Weakness

As odd as it may sound, we've learned that some people choose not to laugh because they feel laughing makes them seem weak or vulnerable. Often the only time these people laugh is when they see something that is damaging or hurtful. The truth is that people like this usually need laughter more than anyone else. Behind their tough masks is the same desire for joy and happiness that you and I have.

I have found in counseling that these tough types of people are simply searching for acceptance and happy relationships. They just don't know how to go about it. They have learned to relate to other people in a negative manner. And unfortunately, they haven't given themselves the freedom to enjoy life and laughter.

If you fit this description, you need to realize that laughter is an important quality that needs to be developed as you travel through life looking for happiness.

DEVELOPING A SENSE OF HUMOR

Laugh at the Little Things in Life

In developing a sense of humor, it is important to be on the lookout for amusing situations. Many funny things happen around us each day. But often we see them as just another source of stress. In reality these "uncomfortable" situations might be very funny.

An example of what I mean is what I have come to call "unmentioned commonalities." These are things that happen all the time but we never talk about them and we rarely even notice when they happen to others. For instance, have you ever noticed that when a person trips while he is walking, he will inevitably look back to see what it was that he tripped over as if to say, "Who did that to me?"

Here's another: For some reason everyone takes bread from the middle of the loaf. They just reach right in the bag to the middle as if the first couple of pieces had something wrong with them. Or how about the uncomfortable situation when you are sitting at a table and your foot touches another foot. You think, "How can I move my foot without her realizing that we were touching?"

These are the little common things that happen to everyone. They may not be laugh-out-loud funny, but they can be very funny if they are viewed in the right way.

Listening to comedians can help a person understand how to make little things funny. Professional comedians are experts in taking the little, ordinary things in life and making them come alive through exaggeration. You don't need to study comedians to develop a sense of humor, but pay attention to their exaggeration and unique angle of seeing things.

Laugh at Yourself
Too many people take life far too seriously. They forget to laugh and love. They are so concerned about building their mountain of personal credentials that they forget to play in the mud puddle at the bottom to maintain their sanity.

When I take myself too seriously (usually when I'm trying to make myself look good), I usually end up doing or saying something really stupid.

"For every one who exalts himself will be humbled, and he who humbles himself will be exalted" (Luke 14:11 RSV).

Jesus also told his followers to become childlike; little children aren't as concerned with making themselves look good as we are.

One thing that I do in my attempt to not take myself too seriously is to carry a picture of myself that is so ridiculous that I have to laugh each time I look at it. Unfortunately, it wasn't very hard for me to find one! But I realize that there is no way I can take myself seriously when I have the potential of looking that bad. I have some photos of myself that are definitely candidates for a web site of goofy-looking people.

If you are too concerned with how you look, you might want to ask yourself, "Am I worrying so much about myself that I'm not focusing on God and what he might have for me today? If God wanted to use me for something great, would I hear him, or am I too loud listening and worrying about myself?"

If you can learn to laugh at yourself in spite of your weakness, then you are on your way to developing a great sense of humor.

Laughter can be an emotional release, very much like tears. Our emotions are more connected than you think. Have you ever laughed so hard you cried? If this natural emotion is used in a positive manner, it can become one of your greatest sources of happiness and overflowing joy. Keep laughing and watch how it makes you live large, be different, and shine bright.

LIVING LARGE TODAY

Use these questions for a time of reflection, as you write in your personal journal, or when you get together with your small group.

1. What kinds of things make you laugh?

2. How do you feel when you make someone laugh?

3. Have you been the subject of misdirected humor or sarcasm? If so, how did it feel?

4. How do you think other people could be pointed to Jesus through laughter?

Here's where it all comes together—these 12 character qualities can be yours with the help and power of God. God does the impossible; you do the possible and watch what happens. When you take time to slow down, pause, and reflect, you'll really become different.

12 REFLECTION
Taking Time to Think About God and Yourself

If you are still holding this book (and if it is open to this chapter) there is a good chance that you are at least a little different than when you first picked it up. This last chapter is our final stop along the road to living large, being different, and shining bright.

As you look around at the people with whom you interact each day, you will see a percentage who seem as though they are always lost. They move quickly from one thing to another trying to find the best deal, trying to make a deal, or trying to be in on a deal. But mostly, they seem intent on keeping busy. In fact, they appear to be driven by the illusion that being busy is a good thing for them. They value busyness so much they even ask the question, "You keeping busy?" as if busyness is a good thing. Busyness isn't a good thing when it steals time from thinking about God and his ways. This has not been an easy lesson for me to learn, and I've come to understand this reality much slower than I would have liked.

Many of us will do almost anything to please people. Unfortunately, trying to please everybody often leads to pleasing nobody. I know of many families who have gone through a painful divorce because work and "busyness" were more important than the marriage and developing the relationships within the family.

I have learned that when I am too busy and my schedule is out of control, I can easily lose sight of my relationship with God. In my years as a pastor, I've seen first-hand that when a follower of Jesus gets over-scheduled, the first thing that suffers is usually his or her alone time with God. Refreshment is replaced by busyness.

As you read this chapter we want you to see that God created the concept of rest, and that rest is both good and needed. Without rest there is little time for reflection and the many great benefits that we receive when we spend time with God and evaluate our life.

God Created Rest

By the seventh day God had finished the work he had been doing; so on the seventh day he rested from all his work. And God blessed the seventh day and made it holy, because on it he rested from all the work of creating that he had done (Genesis 2:2-3 NIV).

God didn't need to rest, because he is God. But he chose to rest and gave us an example to follow.

Resting gives us time to reflect on what we have been doing. When the body slows down, the mind follows. It also offers relaxation and refreshment from all of the activity we have been involved in.

Jesus Rested

Although Jesus was 100 percent God, he was also 100 percent human and rested on various occasions. He only had a few years of ministry on earth, yet he frequently took time to reflect on what he had been doing and to communicate with his Father.

As someone who knows busy as well as ministry, I would think Jesus would want to do all that he could and spend all of his waking hours ministering to and healing people. There was so much to do and he had such a short time on earth. Yet Jesus didn't live that way. He took needed rest time from his busy schedule (see Mark 6:46-47).

WHEN WE ARE TOO BUSY

We Miss Out on the Small Things in Life

Our society usually equates big with beautiful, but some of the most beautiful things on this great planet are small. When we are too busy we tend to pass the small things by without much thought. Before I was married, I had the opportunity to live in a large beach house that was 15 feet from the bay. Every morning I woke up to the stillness of the bay as it stretched out past the jetty and into the ocean. Boats, birds, and jumping fish would regularly put on a show that I would watch from my bedroom window. It was a beautiful—but the longer I lived there, the less I appreciated it. It wasn't until I got married and moved into a small apartment in the middle of the city that I began to miss the small beauties of the ocean. I'm glad it didn't take me longer to realize that the small things in this world are both beautiful and important.

This poem seems to say exactly what I mean:

If I had my life to live over again, I'd try to make more mistakes next time.
I would relax, I would limber up, I would be sillier than I have been this trip.
I know of very few things I would take seriously.
I would take more trips. I would be crazier.
I would climb more mountains, swim more rivers, and watch more sunsets.
I would do more walking and looking.
I would eat more ice cream and less beans.
I would have more actual troubles, and fewer imaginary ones.
You see, I'm one of those people who lives life sensibly and sanely hour after hour, day after day. I've been one of those people who never go anywhere without a thermometer, a hot-water bottle, a gargle, a raincoat, aspirin, and a parachute.

If I had to do it over again I would go places,
do things, and travel lighter than I have.
If I had my life to live over I would start bare-
footed earlier in the spring and stay that
way later in the fall.
I would play hookey more.
I wouldn't make such good grades, except by accident.
I would ride on more merry-go-rounds. I'd pick more daisies. [4]

May this poem be a challenge for you to slow down and see
and experience some of the small things God has given us.

What about you? What "small things" are you missing out on?

We Miss Out on Knowing Ourselves

We desperately need time alone to reflect on where we have been and
how we have interacted with our world. We need to evaluate our actions
and ask ourselves thoughtful questions about the situations we have
been in to see if we really did the right thing. In this way we can learn
from our victories as well as from our failures. Finding out whom we
really are takes time, but you won't have time if you're always busy. As
with any discipline, you have to practice; if you want to improve yourself
as a person, you must set aside time to reflect. But where do you find
the time?

I use the time as I drive to work or from one place to another to get in
touch with my thoughts and feelings. I used to hate to drive until I gave
this time to myself to think and reflect on where I have been, my feelings,
my relationship with God, and my relationships with others. Now, I find
that I look forward to driving—without the radio. Sometimes, I even take
the long way to get where I have to go. When do you take time to be by
yourself and reflect on who you really are? If you don't currently do this,
when can you?

We Miss Out on Knowing God

God wants to spend time with us, yet when we don't take time to reflect on who he is and how he is active in our lives, we tend to lose the closeness that we should experience with him. We settle for second best because we give him second best.

Here's how one person described his relationship with God:

> I would like to buy $3 worth of God, please, not enough to explode my soul or disturb my sleep, but just enough to equal a cup of warm milk or a snooze in the sunshine. I don't want enough of him to make me love a black man or pick beets with a migrant. I want ecstasy, not transformation; I want the warmth of the womb, not a new birth. I want a pound of the eternal in a paper sack. I would like to buy $3 worth of God, please. [5]

Not enough of God to really change him—how sad!

The psalmist wrote the following challenge: *Be still, and know that I am God (Psalm 46:10 NIV).* If you aren't setting aside time to be quiet and think about God and his ways and your life, there's a good chance you are asking for only three dollars worth of him. Be challenged to spend time with God knowing that he looks forward to this time to become close and to refresh you.

PRACTICAL SUGGESTIONS FOR REFLECTION

Find a Quiet Spot

So often we are surrounded by music, television, and other distracting noises that make it difficult to enjoy quietness. Find a spot in or near your house that you know will be quiet and where you can retreat to for time to reflect. Use this time to be quiet and listen for God to speak to you in your heart and thoughts.

When I was in college, there was an abandoned tree swing near my apartment. I would retreat to that swing when I needed extended time to be alone. To this day when I visit that area, I return to that swing because of the great memories I have of the time spent there with God.

Start a Journal

Find any type of folder and begin to write down the thoughts, dreams, and goals you think of during your quiet time. I use a cheap 40-page spiral notebook so I can buy a new one every other month or so and because it makes me feel as if I have room to write as much as I want. Here are examples of two entries that I wrote recently:

Nov. 8th: Today I felt like the only time that God was in my life was when I drove by the church. I had a lousy day, God. I really want to please you and be the person that you want me to be but I'm struggling with who I am and my communication with you...sorry. I love you though.

Nov. 13th: This morning I feel great about myself! I got good sleep and after playing an hour of basketball I feel real good. I know this is going to be a great day. God, teach me something new today and make me sensitive to those that I come in contact with. Thanks God for my body and the abilities that you have given me. Forgive me when I often take these things for granted. Thanks for loving me!

There is no one way that everyone must do in order to reflect in a journal. You have the freedom to write whatever you want. No one else needs to see what you write. I try to write more of my feelings and thoughts, which forces me to really think. One of my favorite journal exercises is to write out what I did yesterday and then slowly reflect on those actions to see if God was trying to teach me something that I was staying too busy to see or moving too fast to catch. I'll often return and reread some of what I wrote and reflect on where I have been, how I have grown, and what I have been through—by returning to my feelings I almost always see how God worked in my life.

Please don't be intimidated by rules or guidelines to writing; just write whatever you want. Let this be your time to freely reflect on you and your God.

Get Away

A "solo" is an exercise where you go away to be by yourself for a specific period of time. I was introduced to this concept of a "solo" when I was a sophomore in high school going to summer camp. I was challenged to try to spend six hours by myself without talking to anyone or listening to music. My initial reaction was, "You've got to be kidding. I could never do that!" But to my surprise, and everyone else's, this forced experience turned out to be everyone's favorite event of the camp. Our group loved it! Many of the people who experienced the solo still incorporate that discipline in their lives today. Give it a try.

Seek Variety

Who says that your time with God has to be the same every day? I know many people get tired of trying to read their Bibles every day. They begin to feel guilty, and then they stop reading it all together. But even if you don't read your Bible every day, you should have daily time with God. Why not make your time with God a creative experience? Write God a letter; think of ways in which he reminds you of something in your room; go outside and look around at his creation and thank him for it; paraphrase an event that happened in the Bible and write it out in your own words; or write out your favorite verse and tell God why you like it. The options are limitless. God wants you to spend time with him, and he would rather have that time be creative than boring or predictable. (If the idea of a creative time with God interests you then you might want to look at p. 119 for a book called *Creative Times with God*.)

Our prayer is that you would spend some time in reflection on all that you have learned in this book, and ask God to begin to change you into his image as you develop and sharpen the skills that we wrote about. Reflect on how you can put into practice some of these qualities in your life as you become the person God created you to be. Remember, God loves you not for what you do, but for who you are.

There are enough "average" people out there. Choose to stand out. Live large! Be different! Shine bright!

If this becomes your goal and your prayer, it will make a huge difference in your life and in the lives of others.

May the words a good friend spoke to me during a time of personal stress and busyness challenge you to learn to be still and know your God:

> *Reduce and master; don't take yourself so seriously. Laugh more, pursue God with reckless abandon, enjoy people, and surprise strangers by occasionally wearing your underwear over your clothes.*

LIVING LARGE TODAY

Use these questions for a time of reflection, as you write in your personal journal, or when you get together with your small group.

1. When was the last time you slowed down, turned off, and reflected on God?

2. Can you think of a spot where you could spend time with God on a regular basis? Why might that be a good spot for you?

3. Why do you—or don't you—journal right now? Do you have an outlet for reflecting?

4. What will be your commitment to change now that you've read this book? Who can hold you accountable and talk to you on a regular basis and encourage you to live large, be different, and shine bright? Pick up the phone right now and call someone to take on that role in your life. You can do it!

NOTES

1. John Powell, Why Am I Afraid to Love? (Allen: Argus Communications, 1967), 104-105.

2. John Powell, Why Am I Afraid to Love? (Allen: Argus Communications, 1967), 12.

3. © Copyright 1984 by LIBRIS MUSIC (A DIV. OF LEXICON MUSIC, INC.) ASCAP All rights reserved. International copyright secured. Used by permission.

4. "I Would Pick More Daisies." Inspirational Stories. © 2005-2010. 5 April 2010. < http://www.great-inspirational-quotes.com/i-would-pick-more-daisies.html>.

5. Charles Swindoll, Improving Your Serve: The Art of Unselfish Living (Waco: Word Books, 1981), 29.